DICTIONARY OF
APHRODISIACS

H. E. WEDECK

DICTIONARY OF
APHRODISIACS

———

H. E. WEDECK

BRACKEN BOOKS
LONDON

Dictionary of Aphrodisiacs

First published in the British Commonwealth
by Peter Owen Ltd in 1962

Copyright © Peter Owen Ltd 1994

This edition published under licence in 1994 by Bracken
Books, an imprint of Studio Editions Ltd, Princess House,
50 Eastcastle Street, London W1N 7AP, England

ISBN 1 85891 129 X

Printed at Thomson Press (I) Ltd

ACKNOWLEDGMENT

For the use of pharmacological matter used in this book, due acknowledgment is made to *Passport to Paradise?*, by Dr. Bernard Finch. New York, Philosophical Library, 1960.

INTRODUCTION

Throughout all ages and at all cultural levels, in court and hovel, among beggars and princelings, one of the dominant forces that have driven men to exultant achievements, triumphant productivity, and personal contentment, is the amatory concept. The gnomic belief that the world is conditioned by love is no idle apothegm. Love, as the instrument of creative agencies and cosmic perpetuity, is no banausic conception. The ancient Roman poet Lucretius, opening his vast poem on the composition of the universe, invokes the amatory divinity as the primal and supreme agent of universal operations:

> O mother of the descendants of Aeneas,
> darling of men and gods, fostering Venus!
> Beneath the gliding stars of heaven you
> throng the sea with ships and fill the
> productive lands. For through you every
> living thing is conceived and rises and beholds
> the light of the sun.

That is no mere poetic tribute, for all human activities pay their obligations to the goddess, symbolically on occasion, more frequently in actuality. In the service of Venus ghastly and unhallowed crimes have been committed, men have braved tempestuous dangers, have renounced magnificence, power, and possessions, confirming the almost thaumaturgic virtue of 'All for love.' So great is the divinity's potency, so urgent the overwhelming passion with which she besets man.

It is therefore not surprising that man has continuously

sought every means, every obscure aid, the most furtive suggestion, to maintain his amorous faculties. For these faculties have invariably been held in the utmost esteem, enshrouded in hieratic mysticism and sanctity, in ancient Greece and Babylonia as well as in India, in the Dark Ages no less than in these frenzied contemporary times. Erotic vigor, in all its varying manifestations, perverted and abnormal, wholesome and acceptable, is the symbol not only of human generation but of man's approximation to supreme creativity. Endowed with this virility, man is the manifestation of the continuity of the human race, of the entire cosmos. Likewise woman becomes the complement in this function. Hence the two harmonizing principles of creation and survival, male and female, run through the entire stream of human history, from proto-historic aeons to the present, like a vibrant, recognizable leitmotif, permeating the creative arts, sculpture and painting, music and literature, without neglecting the basic, simpler doings of the ordinary man and woman.

> What would not a man give if he
> might converse with Orpheus and
> Musaeus and Hesiod and Homer?
> Nay, if this be true, let me die
> again and again.

These are the words of Socrates in Plato's *Apology*. In the pursuit of the amatory virtues, in the eternal desire to retain or recover that potency, man's aspiration has been no less, in its own way, than the longing of Socrates.

Virility has always been one of the most dominant and most desirous characteristics of the human male. Notably in ancient times, in Greek and Roman cultures, in the Middle East, in the Orient. And at all times, now as in proto-history, the membrum virile is the symbol of creation, the ultimate basis and source of life. Hence the cult of the phallus, whether by indirection or as a forthright and acknowledged rite, has, in the course of centuries, assumed cosmic, divine proportions. In sculpture and in the drama, in Aristophanic farce and in hieratic rituals, in pictorial art and in the stream of literature, the phallus is transcendent. Thus the Priapean poetry of the ancients, particularly of the Romans, hymned sexual potency. Hence the ubiquity of Priapus himself as a sculptural representative of the generative principle, populated the Roman gardens, assertive in ithyphallic pose. The Caves of Ajanta, the medieval Courts of Love, the epithalamia of the erotic poets, Mayan and Incan and Polynesian tribal mores all testify to the glorification of manhood, the supremacy of the sex motif.

To the Greeks, the phallus was never a shameful, obscene object but an awesome and sacred symbol of the cosmic character of the process of generation. Nakedness, therefore, in gymnastic contests, at public national games, in temple rites and at dances, involved no personal shame, no public offensiveness. To the Romans, however, total denudation was a matter of condemnation. An old poet, Ennius, writes,
Shame begins with public nakedness.

Virility is sustained, preserved, even recaptured, by man's ingenuities, by exotic foods and drinks, by rare herbal compounds, by fantastic manipulations, goetic periapts. Even the putatively innocuous whimsical shapes and designs of cakes and pastry, notably in Central Europe, retain to this day the phallic concept, the cryptic induration of the aphrodisiac function.

In modern times the external trappings of phallicism are not, as a rule, so visually evident. Yet the passionate interest in the subject is all pervasive. Aphrodite in the function of Astarte is triumphant. A eunuch is a negative creature. A beardless Moslem is contemptuously designated as manless. Sexual virility, coital potency rides high and arrogant over the commercial, artistic, social strivings of contemporary society, and, equally, but in varying degree, in the social frame of any age. The universal clamor has always been for the most efficacious means of retaining or restoring the sexual faculties.

This book surveys and classifies the means, herbal and scientific, legendary, medicinal and culinary, that man has taken, through the ages and under disparate circumstances, to perpetuate or to extend his masculinity, his functional operations, against the challenges of oncoming age or decrepitude or the multiple assaults of exhaustion.

H.E.W.

DICTIONARY OF APHRODISIACS

A

Absinthe

A liqueur made in France from Artemisia Absinthium. This is a bushy plant with silky stems and small yellow flowers. It grows in waste areas, under hedges, near ditches, in North Africa and in the foothills and valleys of the mountain ranges of Europe.

Absinthe, which is manufactured from the plant, is a green liqueur, compounded of marjoram, oil of aniseed, and other aromatic oils. The use of absinthe is dangerous.

Artemisia absinthium, known as wormwood, was used anciently to banish demons. Hence it was associated with the rites of St. John's Eve, when a crown of the plant was made from its sprays for apotropaic purposes, to ward off malefic spirits.

Tradition credits John the Baptist with wearing a girdle, fashioned of wormwood, while he was in the wilderness.

Wormwood was dedicated to the ancient Greek goddess Diana, who was also called Artemis—hence the name of the herb Artemisia.

Dioscorides, the Greek physician of the first century A.D., was familiar with the plant. He declared that it prevents intoxication.

In England the plant is called Green Ginger and Old Woman.

Although absinthe has been considered a sexual stimulant, when taken in large quantities it leads to insanity.

It must not be used without proper medical advice.

Achilles Tatius

A rhetorician of Alexandria, of the fourth century A.D.

Author of the love romance of Cleitophon and Leucippe. In addition to the central love theme, it contains strange discussions on the nature of love, in a variety of forms.

Books such as this romance were popularly considered as indirect stimulants to amatory experiences. This attitude was prevalent particularly in later ages, notably in Italy during the Renaissance, when erotic fiction became a kind of perfumed aphrodisiac and the courts of dukes and princelings, the palaces of courtiers and the salons of professional ladies echoed with such tales.

Boccaccio's *Decameron* is merely an imaginative, creative evocation of a not too disparate reality.

Acorus Calamus

An aromatic herb, called in the Middle Ages Sweet Flag. In ancient Roman days it was associated with erotic practices and was known as Venus' plant.

Action of Aphrodisiacs

In varying degrees, they heighten desire and facilitate the amatory consummation. But it must again be stressed that aphrodisiacs are in a large measure of traditional interest in the progression of human culture, and that their use generally involves grave hazards and must not be put in practice without due medical advice.

Even from an academic viewpoint, however, it is amazing to note the lengths—sometimes involving serious physiological disturbances and even fatality—to which man can go in his unresolved quest.

Adrenaline

This drug, used in treating asthma, is said to have occasional aphrodisiac effects. This is also the case with the other drugs that stimulate the sympathetic nervous system, ephedrine and amphetamine sulphate or Benzedrine.

These drugs, however, should not be used without medical supervision.

2

Advertisements

The search for sexual vigor, at all age levels and in all social strata is so intense and so pervasive that the periodical press, particularly the popular magazines, is eagerly scanned for advice, advertisements, panaceas on the subject. Charms, pills, ointments and other concoctions flood the market for this purpose. In one monthly magazine an "occultist by powerful magical ceremony prepares a Glyph Talisman for 'LOVE.'" The price per wish is $6.00. The advertiser is B.M. Asmodeus. Note that in Hebraic legend and in occultism Asmodeus is King of the Demons.

The popular magazines, especially in the English-speaking countries, regularly contain advertisements that are virtually of a visual aphrodisiac nature.

Aelius

An Alexandrian physician of the second century A.D. He recommended the flesh of the lizard to ensure virility.

See *LIZARD*.

Affion

This was a Chinese preparation, of which the chief ingredient was opium. It was asserted that its erotic effect was violent and brutal.

Africa

In early days, in Africa, the lacerta scincus, an amphibious animal of the lizard species, was commonly used, ground into a powder, as a powerful aphrodisiac.

Agate

Like a great many other stones, precious and semi-precious, the agate has a putative reputation for stimulating amorous activity.

In the Middle Ages in particular great trust was placed in the efficacy of such stones, in the sense that they possessed talismanic virtues.

3

Agnus Castus

Also called the Chaste-tree and Abraham's Balm. A tree whose leaves were anciently reputed to produce an anti-aphrodisiac effect. Pliny the Elder, the Roman author of the *Historia Naturalis,* and Dioscorides, the first century A.D. Greek army physician, author of *Materia Medica,* mention that, during a certain Greek festival called the Thesmophoria, agnus was strewn over the bed by married women.

The thistle was also reputed to have this anti-aphrodisiac property.

Aischrologia

The frank expression of obscenities. This type of expression was common in ancient Greek comedy, particularly in Aristophanes. Aischrologia is an indirect amatory stimulus.

The contemporary drama and also fiction, both European and American, have in recent years broken all barriers of literary and verbal restraints and have incorporated this aischrological technique as possibly a challenge to traditional mores and also as an avant-garde manifesto of a newer, franker attitude toward the actualities of life.

Literary instances of this moment are James Joyce's *Ulysses* and D.H. Lawrence's *Lady Chatterley's Lover.*

Whatever their basic purpose, whatever their literary values, they contain verbal matter of an at least indirect aphrodisiac nature.

Albertus Magnus

This medieval philosopher and occultist, in the course of his many varied works, offers numerous formulas for love-potions. He particularly recommends the brains of a partridge calcined into a powder and swallowed in red wine.

Alchemical Aphrodisiac

In the Middle Ages the alchemists sold a putative aphrodisiac of which gold itself was a reputed ingredient.

The preparation was in the form of a beverage, and was to be taken daily as "potable gold."

4

Alcibiades

A famous Greek political leader of the fifth century B.C. His amorous tendencies were so urgent that on his coat of arms there was the design of Eros, god of love, hurling lightning. The historian Diogenes Laërtius, who flourished in the third century A.D., says that Alcibiades, when a young man, separated wives from their husbands.

Alcohol

Alcohol, with sugar added, was used to promote the amorous feelings of King Louis XIV. In some European countries it was a folk custom to offer a bride and bridegroom cakes moistened with sugar and alcohol.

In small amounts, alcohol removes inhibitions by depressing the "higher centres" of the brain. Sexual desire may be increased but the consummation is negligible or abortive.

Biblical literature contains frequent references to the use of alcohol, but moderation at all times is stressed,

It is not for kings, O Lemuel, it is not for kings to drink wine, nor for princes strong drink. Lest they drink, and forget the law, and prevent the judgment of any of the afflicted. Give strong drink unto him that is ready to perish and wine unto those that be of heavy hearts. Let him drink, and forget his poverty, and remember his misery no more.

Rom. 14. 21.

Algolagnia

A term that includes the two sexual perversions of masochism and sadism.

See *MARQUIS DE SADE, MASOCHISM.*

Almonds

An aphrodisiac preparation, described by Nefzawi in *The Perfumed Garden,* is as follows,

A glassful of very thick honey, eat twenty almonds and one hundred grains of the pine tree before bedtime. Continue for three successive days.

Almond Soup

Powdered almonds, with yolk of eggs, chicken stock, and cream. According to Norman Douglas, this soup has a good aphrodisiac potential.

In many cases, such recipes are basically wholesome and hence induce a feeling of well-being. This physiological state is itself not militant against erotic expression.

Amanita Muscaria

A substance that produces hallucinations, like mescaline, and also induces sexual intensities, with corresponding heightening of sensory channels, and the olfactory and visual senses, and a general condition of a kind of love intoxication.

This hallucinogenic drug is dangerous and must not be used without proper medical or psychiatric controls.

Amatory Cooking

Among foods and dishes that are reputed to have promotive aphrodisiac virtues are, beef curry, onion soup, soft herring roe, cheese soup, egg omelette, chicken curry, fritters made of apples, pears, pineapples, also milk puddings, herrings, oyster stew.

As a rule, such foods, wholesome in themselves, are conducive to a feeling of euphoria. This feeling in turn may well promote, it is regularly suggested, amorous encounters.

Amatory Intensity

Ovid, the Roman poet, describes the intensity of kissing as a preliminary aphrodisiac. In his *Amores* he says,

I saw their frenzied kisses, linking tongue with tongue.

Other means of provoking erotic conditions are also described, these are virtually visual aphrodisiacs, speaking with expressive eyebrows, gesturing, making conversation with the eyes, expressing love with the lips.

Amatory Manoeuvres

Dr. Jacobus mentions, among Oriental aberrations, some

6

Chinese obscene practices whose significance must be retained in their Latin form,

mordere dorsum,
ut gallus facere coitum,
volutare in sterculinio
See *JACOBUS.*

Amatory Plant

The *Geneanthropoeia* mentions a plant, without naming it, that grows on the Atlas Mountains. It has the property of arousing erotic expression.

Likewise Scaliger, a medieval scholar, mentions a tree, without naming it, that is indigenous to India and has marked aphrodisiac properties.

See *GENEANTHROPOEIA.*

Amazons

According to Eustathius, the twelfth century historian and scholar, the ancient Amazons had the strange custom of breaking the leg or arm of any captive taken in battle. The intention was not to prevent the possibility of escape, but to render the captive more vigorous for amatory conflicts, as the Amazons imagined that the genital members would be strengthened by the deprivation of one of the captive's extremities, whether leg or arm. Hence, when reproached by the Scythians with the limping gait of her slaves, Queen Antianara replied, "The lame best perform the act of love."

Ambergris

A waxy substance found in tropical seas, believed to be the secretion in the intestines of the sperm whale. Used in cooking as an aphrodisiac.

In seventeenth century France courtiers and roués customarily nibbled chocolates covered with ambergris. Madame du Barry used ambergris as a perfume to retain the affection of Louis XV.

Among the Persians, pastilles consisting of powdered ambergris, rubies, gold, pearls were eaten as an aphrodisiac.

In the Orient ambergris is at the present time considered as a potent aphrodisiac. Coffee is often served with a little ambergris at the bottom of the cup. According to one authority, three grains of ambergris are sufficient to produce, along with other effects, a disposition to cheerfulness and venereal desires.

It was also claimed to be a medicament that could, for a short time, restore youth to senility.

Among the ancients, ambergris was so used as a restorative of vital powers that had been exhausted by age or excess.

In the East, this perfume still maintains a reputation for life-preserving qualities.

Ambologera

The postponer of old age. This name is applied to the goddess Aphrodite in her capacity as an animating agent. Prayers were addressed to this deity by those interested in retaining vigor or in acquiring rejuvenescence.

The Roman poet Martial alludes to this in an epigram,

Suppliantly he begs, both for himself and for two miserable persons: make this one young, O Cytherean goddess, and this one make virile.

Amoreux, P. J.

A French naturalist and physician of the early nineteenth century. Author of *Opuscule sur Les Truffes,* a translation from the Latin of a certain sixteenth century Alphonsus Cicarellus. The subject is the value, both gastronomic and amatory, of truffles.

See *TRUFFLES.*

Amorous Inducement

In giving amatory advice to Romans, the poet Ovid, in his *Ars Amatoria,* emphasizes a number of points that favor erotic conditions, a sun-tan, cleanliness, neat dress, brushed teeth, well fitting sandals, a good haircut.

In the case of women, Ovid suggests, an elegant coiffure, dress that is becoming to the wearer's shape and complexion, a graceful gait, well-controlled laughter when the occasion arises. Erotically, Ovid advises aggressiveness. Love hates laziness, he warns.

Amorous Supper

Brillat-Savarin, the nineteenth century French gourmet and author of *La Physiologie du Goût,* tells a story in which amatory expression was violently manifested as a result of a dinner that included game and truffles.

Anacharsis

A seventh century B.C. Hellenized philosopher, to whom is traditionally ascribed the injunction,

Restrain the tongue, the stomach, the *membrum virile.*

Anacyclus Pyrethrum

This plant, also called Pellitory of Spain, is used medicinally. It has also, according to a famous Arab erotologist, aphrodisiac properties.

Anaesthetics

Some anaesthetics, such as ether and chloroform, may induce, during a surgical operation, marked erotic fantasies of almost realistic intensity. But these are side issues, and anaesthetics, as an amatory procedure, should never be administered.

Analeptic Diet

For promotion of the secretion of the semen virile, an analeptic diet is recommended by one writer. Such food, without fatiguing the gastric organs, he asserts, furnishes an abundant chyle, from which is elaborated a rich blood, and in which the secretory organs find materials of excellent quality. All food of easy and quick digestion is an analeptic food. A man who adopts this food becomes consequently very well fitted to make the sacrifices exacted by the calls of love.

This is epitomized from the nineteenth century erotologist John Davenport.

Analgesic Effect of Mandrake

Apart from its associations with amatory practices, the mandrake was often used, particularly in ancient times, in order to stupefy criminals who had been sentenced to crucifixion.

In the fifth century A.D., Theodoric, King of the Ostrogoths, used mandrake in a wine decoction, when preparing victims for crucifixion.

The Greek satirist Lucian also alludes to the dulling effect of the mandrake potion,

Do you think he had been so drugged with mandragora as to hear those things and not to know?

Analogous Aphrodisiacs

Often, through the ages, plants and various herbs, by their pseudo-similarity in form, or by a symbolic resemblance to the human genitalia, or suggestive of genital secretions, have been associated with aphrodisiac qualities, as, for instance, in the case of the mandrake.

See *MANDRAKE*.

Ananga-Ranga

A Sanskrit manual similar in content to Ovid's *Ars Amatoria*. Written by Kalyanamalla.

This guide has been translated into a number of Indian languages and also into English by Sir Richard Burton.

It deals with a vast area of amatory techniques, cosmetic and beautifying hints, aphrodisiac prescriptions, magic ointments for securing and retaining affection and love, in the case of both men and women, perfumes, bodily hygiene, hair

10

treatments, drugs, philtres, pills, incense, periapts and charms designed for erotic subjugation, magic incantations for the purpose of fascination, lingam and yoni hints.

Anaphrodisia
The absence of the productive powers. Such a condition may be, in some cases, organically physiological, and in other cases the result of lesions and injuries of various kinds.

Anaphrodisiac
Excessive indulgence in spirituous liquors and wine acts as an anaphrodisiac. This condition is constantly mentioned in Hindu texts, but it is also familiar to the ancient classical writers.

See *WINE*.

Tobacco and the plant valerian are also considered to be anaphrodisiac in their effects, diminishing sexual inclination. Also vinegar, dried coriander, potassium bromide, cocaine, vervain, acid drinks, lemonade.

Among the ancient Greeks, before the festival of the Thesmophoria, women had to abstain from sexual indulgence for nine days. As an aid, they covered their beds with certain leaves and herbs that had cooling effects. Among these herbs was *agnus castus*, that is now known as *chaste-tree* and *Abraham's Balm*. In addition, the women ate garlic, whose unpleasant odor dissuaded men from approach.

Anaphrodisiac Plants
Among this group are the solanacei alkaloids, that have a decided anti-sexual tendency. Such plants and similar anaphrodisiacs were often used, especially in the Middle Ages, to promote asceticism and, in the case of monks, to diminish fleshly desires.

Anaxarchus
A Greek friend of Alexander the Great. He used to have

11

his wine poured out for him by a young naked beautiful girl. It was a form of homage to Bacchus and to Eros. It was at the same time a form of visual aphrodisiac, characteristic of the ancient Greek symposia.

Through the ages, secret clubs and private banquets have presented similar techniques. In fiction, the novels of the Marquis de Sade contain lavish descriptions of such scenes.

See *MARQUIS DE SADE*.

Anchovies

In Southern European countries, they have long been reputed to be lust-provoking.

If nothing more, they are gastronomically appealing.

Ancient Experiments

The ancients, including the Greeks and the Romans, were interested in finding out which plants made people fall in love with each other.

Thus, in the course of time, there grew up an immense corpus of sexual knowledge, some of it based on hearsay, poetic imagery, and wild legend, some of it, again, resulting from observation and more effective testing.

This knowledge was extended, adapted, occasionally misinterpreted, and applied with various local and national modifications so that, in the Middle Ages, an immense sexual awareness lay within the common domain throughout the European continent, spreading Eastward and mingling with the even older knowledge that the Orient possessed. It was, to a large degree, a confused amorphous mass of facts and fantastic beliefs, hopeful and wishful prescriptions, barbarous operations, mystic and sometimes sinister and dangerous recommendations. It was misunderstood information, overladen with superstitious credence, with alchemical exaggerations, with astrological formularies, with magic undertones. But, offering strange and exultant prizes, it was eagerly accepted on its face value by all those who hauntingly, panting,

12

lustfully or pitifully were in search of an elixir, the panacea for senility, the periapt for potency in an amatory sense.

Angel Water
First used by the Portuguese. Popular in the eighteenth century. Shake together a pint of orange flower water, a pint of rose water, a half pint of myrtle water. Add two thirds of distilled spirit of musk, and two thirds of spirit of ambergris. A reputed aphrodisiac aid.

Animal Genitalia
The membrum of the stag was credited with furnishing a man with an abundance of vital fluid, possibly because the stag itself was considered the most salacious of animals.

It was recorded that the Tartars used to entertain the same views in respect of the horse. A French writer, Foucher d'Obsonville, describes such an instance,

Les palefreniers amènent un cheval de sept à huit ans, mais nerveux, bien nourri et en bon état. On lui présente une jument comme pour la saillir, et cependant on le retient de façon à bien irriter ses idées. Enfin, dans le moment où il semble qu'il va lui être libre de s'élancer dessus, l'on fait adroitement passer la verge dans un cordon dont le noeud coulant est rapproché au ventre, ensuite, saisissant à l'instant où l'animal paraît dans sa plus forte érection, deux hommes qui tiennent les extrémités du cordon le tirent avec force et, sur le champ, le membre est séparé du corps au dessus du noeud coulant. Par ce moyen, les esprits sont retenus et fixés dans cettes partie laquelle reste gonflée; aussitôt on la lave et la fait cuire avec divers aromatiques et épiceries aphrodisiaques.

Animals
In *The Perfumed Garden*, Nefzawi digressively but interestingly discusses, in great and curious detail, the

13

amorous activities of animals. In a sense, he is the prototype, in the Arabic field, of Ferdinand Fabre.

See *PERFUMED GARDEN*.

Anise

A plant indigenous to the Eastern Mediterranean area. Used as a sexual stimulant as a culinary ingredient.

In the latter sense it has acquired a reputation among gourmets.

Annamites

Dr. Jacobus, in his anthropological studies, declares that the Annamites were believed to be particularly lascivious on account of their fish-eating habits. In addition, garlic, onion, and ginger entered commonly into their diet.

See *JACOBUS*.

Anthropology

Anthropological studies have appreciably increased knowledge of human mores and aberrations, particularly the researches of Sir Richard Burton, and, much more recently, the investigations of primitive savage life by such anthropologists as Malinowski and Margaret Mead.

A mine of rare research, encyclopedic in scope, is the *Untrodden Fields of Anthropology,* by Dr. Jacobus X. It ranges over several continents, and contains valuable matter on racial peculiarities, erotic mores, amatory practices, exotic social traditions.

Anthropophagous Aphrodisiac

In the desperate search for amatory satisfactions, the most monstrous ingredients have, throughout the ages, been sought and compounded into electuaries and pastilles, philtres and ointments. In the Middle Ages, for instance, a recipe for sex stimulation required the putrefied flesh of a human corpse, together with both human and animal testes and ovaries, pimento, and alcohol.

14

Anti-Aphrodisiac Prescriptions

The two following prescriptions were formerly considered of great efficacy in diminishing the libido,

(1) Da verbena in potu, et non erigitur virga sex diebus.

(2) Utere mentha sicca cum aceto, genitalia illinita succo hyoscyami aut cicutae coitus appetitum sedant.

Anti-Aphrodisiac Recommendations

Water-purslan, cucumbers, even a drink of water have all been estimated, at various times, to be conducive to anti-aphrodisiac feelings. Also a spare diet, a laborious life, little sleep, and much bodily exercise, according to an erotological authority.

In *Othello,* Shakespeare suggests, A sequester from liberty, fasting and prayer, Much castigation, exercise devout.

The ancients also recommended a cool regimen for this purpose. The Greek philosophers, for instance, Plato and Aristotle, advised going barefoot as a means of checking the stimulus to carnal pleasure. The cold bath was considered equally efficacious. Others, including Pliny the Elder, author of the *Historia Naturalis,* and the physician Galen, the second century A.D. Greek authority whose reputation extended far into the Middle Ages, advised thin sheets of lead to be worn on the calves of the legs and near the kidneys.

Sir Thomas Browne, the seventeenth century writer, suggested,

He that is chaste and continent, not to impair his strength, or terrified by contagion, will hardly be heroically virtuous. Adjourn not that virtue until those years when Cato could lend out his wife, and impotent satyrs write satires against lust—but be chaste in thy flaming days, when Alexander dared not trust his eyes upon the fair sisters of Darius, and when so many men think that there is no other way than that of Origen.

See *ORIGEN.*

Anti-Aphrodisiacs

To counterbalance excessive sexual activity, anti-aphrodisiacs have frequently been the object of search. According to the Roman poet Ovid's *Remedia Amoris,* avoidance of idleness is a means of subduing sexual tendencies, whether mental or physical.

Venus otia amat—Venus loves idleness, warns the poet.

If you seek an end to love, be active, you will be safe. . . . Take up law . . . or busy yourself with agriculture . . . or hunting . . . or fishing . . . magic rites are useless.

Again,

Think of your love's faults and defects, avoid solitude. Shun loving couples, shun public groups, public performances and shows.

And avoid certain aphrodisiac foods, such as onions and rockets.

In a general sense, intense mental study, neurotic anxiety, fasting, excessive sleep, snuff taking have all been at various times considered detrimental to amatory activity.

Nicolas Venette similarly advises abstention from erotically inflammatory scenes, study, work, wakefulness, avoidance of obscene paintings and books.

See *VENETTE.*

The seeds and roots of the water lily are likewise considered a preventive against lechery. Apothecaries made a soothing syrup that banished veneral inclinations and lustful thoughts. Among the Turks the water lily was an ingredient as a cooling drink.

Antiochus

This third century B.C. ruler, son of King Seleucus, is reputed to have had such intensely sensitive amatory reactions that the mere name of his mistress, spoken aloud, sent him into a paroxysm.

Many medical case histories describe similar conditions.

16

Ants

A medieval aphrodisiac recipe, that appears in Sinibaldus, contained dried black ants. Oil was poured over them and they were enclosed in a glass jar, ready for use.

See *GENEANTHROPOEIA*.

Antwerp

Many ancient European cities somehow clung to old pagan rites and associations. In Antwerp, for instance, as late as the sixteenth century Priapus was the tutelary god of the city.

Anvalli

A sexual stimulant mentioned in the Hindu erotic manual *Ananga-Ranga*. It consists of the outer shell of the anvalli nut, from which the juice is extracted. Dried in the sun, this juice is mixed with powder of the same nut. The compound is eaten with candied sugar, ghee or clarified butter, and honey.

Apadravyas

In Hindu erotology, these are objects of various kinds and designs, mostly metallic, that are used in connection with amatory relations. They are primarily intended for ithyphallic purposes.

Aphrodisia

A popular Greek festival held in honor of the goddess Aphrodite, patroness of love. At this festival prostitutes and hetairae, a euphemistic name for amatory companions, participated.

At the busy harbor of Corinth, constantly crowded with sailors and seamen, the festival was celebrated with the greatest sexual license, the women causing provocation by dress, speech, and gesture.

This festival and similar ceremonials and rites prevalent in ancient times amply demonstrate the universality of the

17

erotic theme and its forthright acceptance as a basic force not only in human life but in the cosmic procreative design as well.

Aphrodisiac Cakes

In ancient Syracuse, cakes were made in the shape of the *pudenda muliebria* and offered in divine sacrificial rites.

Such pastry, designed to represent the lingam and the yoni, was a common medieval tradition, notably in Teutonic baking.

The custom is far from obsolete.

Aphrodisiac Device

In ancient Sparta, a bride was subjected to a feigned ceremony of ravishment, as the biographer Plutarch recounts, "The wedding itself took place in this manner. Every man carried off a maiden, but not a young one nor one under age for marriage, but one who was fully grown up and marriageable. The so-called bridesmaid received the maiden who had been carried off, shaved her head close, and put on her a man's dress and shoes—laid her on a bed of straw and left her alone in the dark. The bridegroom then crept in secretly, neither drunk nor weakened by dissipation, but quite sober, and after he had, as always, taken a meal with his table-companions, loosed her girdle and lifted her on to the bed. After he had spent a short time with her, he went away again quietly, to sleep in the usual place in the company of the other young men. He did the same thing again and again; he spent the day with his comrades, slept with them at night, and visited his bride only secretly and with circumspection, feeling ashamed and being afraid that someone in her house might see him.

"Yet the bride herself assisted in this, and always knew how to arrange that they might be able to come together at the right time and without being seen. This did they not merely for a short time, but many of them had children born to them, before they had seen their wife by day. Such meetings served not only to make them practise restraint and moderation, but also promoted the birth of children and caused them to embrace with ever fresh and rejuvenated love, so that, instead of becoming sated or weakened by too frequent enjoyment, they left behind as it were a provocative and fuel of mutual love and inclination."

Aphrodisiac Dinner

Such a meal, characterized by great abundance of courses and dishes and drinks that were reputed to have potent erotic effects, is described by the Marquis de Sade in his *120 Journées de Sodome*. The repast, lavishly served, included bisque, twenty hors d'oeuvres, twenty entrées, followed by twenty more, poultry, game garnished and shaped fantastically, roasts, pastries hot and cold, dessert, hot-house fruit, ices, chocolate, liqueurs, burgundy, three different Italian wines, Rhine and Rhône wines, champagne, two Greek wines.

A plenteous meal, asserts the Marquis, may produce voluptuous sensations, le bon dîner peut causer une volupté physique.

Other writers who, like the Marquis de Sade, have observed the close relation between foods and the amatory exercise are the notorious Casanova (1725-1798), who has much to say on this subject in his own *Mémoires,* the French erotic novelist Restif de la Bretonne (1734-1806), author of *La Fille Naturelle, Les Nuits de Paris, La Paysanne Pervertie,* and some three hundred similar tales, Crébillon Fils (1707-1777), whose licentious stories include *L'Ecumoire* and *Les Egarements du Couer,* Andrea de Nerciat (1739-1801), soldier and author of equally licentious novels such as *Montrose* and *Felicia.*

Aphrodisiac Effectiveness

It must be observed that wholesome and recommended items having an aphrodisiac value may be effective generally only when there are no serious organic lesions or functional disturbances.

Such wholesome recipes, containing acceptable food values, produce a certain euphoria, which in itself releases frustrations and restraints and hence encourages amatory activities.

Aphrodisiac Enticements

The Greek hetairae, to increase their enticing charms, used at every possible opportunity to enhance their amatory attractiveness. Hair was dyed black. Grease-paint, false hair, colored ribbons were used as additional adornments. The hetairae were also familiar with eye-paint, seaweed paint, white lead, hair nets and girdles, combs and necklaces, earrings and becoming robes, buckles on arms, rings and jewels.

In addition, the hetairae were taught by professional beldames how to conduct themselves, how to inspire jealousy, how to dress provokingly, how to increase their income, and how to extract the utmost profit from their fleeting beauty.

Aphrodisiac Movement

In ancient Greek comedy the swaying and writhing of the female body, as an erotic excitation, induced comment on the author's part. The feminine practice was known as periproktian.

Aphrodisiac Ointment

In Hindu erotology, a suggested ointment is compounded as follows, flowers of the nauclia cadamba, hog plum, and eugenia jambreana.

In many cases, aphrodisiac recipes fail in specifying exact methods of application or administration. In other cases, again, particularly in Oriental prescriptions, herbal and analogous ingredients may be difficult to identify and to procure.

Aphrodisiac Pill

A Chinese pill intended to augment virile capacity. It is described by the Orientalist and anthropologist Sir Richard Burton as rhubarb colored, and enclosed in a wax capsule.

PLATE 1—*Chefs d'oeuvre d'art au Luxembourg*, S. Montrosier, Paris: Baschet, 1881
Childhood of Bacchus by J. V. Ranvier

The composition of the pill consists of vegetable extracts and vegetable matter. Dissolved in water, it was applied to the generative member.

Aphrodisiac Powder

A beautifying, rejuvenating, and aphrodisiac powder is thus described in Ben Jonson's (c. 1573-1637) *Volpone*.

Volpone, Lady, I kiss your bounty, and for this timely grace you have done your poor Scoto of Mantua, I will return you, over and above my oil, a secret of that high and inestimable nature, shall make you for ever enamored on that minute, wherein your eye descended on so mean, yet not altogether to be despised, an object. Here is a powder concealed in this paper, of which, if I should speak to the worth, nine thousand volumes were but as one page, that page as a line, that line as a word; so short is this pilgrimage of man (which some call life) to the expressing of it. Would I reflect on the price? Why, the whole world is but as an empire, that empire as a province, that province as a bank, that bank as a private purse to the purchase of it. I will only tell you; it is the powder that made Venus a goddess (given her by Apollo), that kept her perpetually young, cleared her wrinkles, firmed her gums, filled her skin, colored her hair; from her derived to Helen, and at the sack of Troy unforunately lost, till now, in this our age, it was as happily recovered, by a studious antiquary, out of some ruins of Asia, who sent a moiety of it to the court of France (but much sophisticated), wherewith the ladies there, now, color their hair. The rest, at this present, remains with me; extracted to a quintessence, so that, wherever it but touches, in youth it perpetually preserves, in age restores the complexion, seats your teeth, did they dance like virginal jacks, firm as a wall.

Aphrodisiacs

By definition, aphrodisiacs imply a stimulus to love. The term is derived from Aphrodite, the Greek goddess in her capacity as a personification of the sexual urge, of generation, of the power of love. To the Greek and Roman poets, Aphrodite is the generative force that pervades the entire cosmos. In his poem *De Rerum Natura* the Roman poet Lucretius invokes the goddess under her Roman name of Venus,

Mother of the descendants of Aeneas, delight of men and gods, O nourishing Venus, beneath the gliding constellations of heaven you fill the sea with sails and the lands with produce, since through you every kind of living creature is conceived, coming forth to gaze upon the light of the sun.

In general, aphrodisiacs involve visual images, olfactory and tactile experiences, physiological operations related to food, drink, drugs, or conceptual pictures inducing libidinous thoughts and impulses. Some so-called aphrodisiacs are, though not effective, at least innocuous, while others may be extremely harmful and dangerous. It is wise, therefore, to take all aphrodisiacs, both figuratively and physiologically, *maximo cum grano salis.*

The efficacy of aphrodisiacs is often a matter of long-standing tradition, untested for validity, but wishfully handed down in oral legend and folktales, in magic rituals and old wives' lore, through the succession of the centuries.

Certain foods and drinks, for example, are traditionally associated with erotic impulses on the mere sequential transmission of such beliefs. But in most of these cases there has been no definitive pharmaceutical or medical approval to warrant such credence. Hence the hopeful persistence of the remedial and restorative measures. What may, however, be asserted categorically is that an abundance of rich and appealing food, reinforced with palatable drinks, all consumed in a pleasant atmosphere in congenial company, will unquestionably induce a feeling of euphoria. This sense of physical and emotional comfort and well-being may well tend toward sensual directions, and the human fallacy has been to deduce, as if logically, a *post hoc* as an *ergo propter hoc.*

It must be understood that throughout this book no

22

advice or recommendation is given as to the actual use of aphrodisiacs, that is a matter for proper medical consultation.

Apart from the putative value of aphrodisiacs, historical or academic interest attaches to the descriptions and traditional properties associated with erotic stimulants.

Rabelais (1490-1553) in his *Gargantua and Pantagruel*, discusses wittily and in detail the subject of aphrodisiacs and anti-aphrodisiacs,

I find in our faculty of medicine, and we have founded our opinion therein upon the deliberate resolution and final decision of the ancient Platonics, that carnal concupiscence is cooled and quelled five different ways.

First, by the means of wine. I shall easily believe that, quoth Friar John, for when I am well whittled with the juice of the grape, I care for nothing else, so I may sleep. When I say, quoth Rondibilis, that wine abateth lust, my meaning is, wine immoderately taken; for by intemperance proceeding from the excessive drinking of strong liquor, there is brought upon the body of such a swill-down bouser, a chillness in the blood, a slackening in the sinews, a dissipation of the generative seed, a numbness and hebetation of the senses, with a perversive wryness and convulsion of the muscles; all of which are great lets and impediments to the act of generation. Hence it is, that Bacchus, the god of bibbers, tipplers, and drunkards, is most commonly painted beardless, and clad in a woman's habit, as a person altogether effeminate, or like a libbed eunuch. Wine, nevertheless, taken moderately, worketh quite contrary effects, as is implied by the old proverb, which saith,—That Venus takes cold, when not accompanied with Ceres and Bacchus. This opinion is of great antiquity, as appeareth by the testimony of Diodorus the Sicilian, and confirmed by Pausanias, and universally held amongst the Lampsacians, that Don Priapus was the son of Bacchus and Venus.

Secondly, The Fervency of lust is abated by certain drugs, plants, herbs, and roots, which make the taker cold, maleficiated, unfit for, and unable to perform the act of generation; as hath been often experimented in the water-lily, Heraclea, Agnus Castus, willow-twigs, hemp-stalks, woodbine, honey-suckle, tamarisk, chaste-tree, mandrake, bennet, keck-bugloss, the skin of a hippopotamus, and many other such, which, by convenient doses proportioned to the peccant humor and constitution of the patient, being duly and seasonably received within the body, what by their elementary virtues on the one side, and peculiar properties on the other,—do either benumb, mortify, and beclumpse with cold the prolific semence, or scatter and disperse the spirits, which ought to have gone along with, and conducted sperm to the places destinated and appointed for its reception,—or lastly, shut up, stop, and obstruct the ways, passages, and conduits through which the seed should have been expelled, evacuated, and ejected. We have nevertheless of those ingredients, which, being of a contrary operation, heat the blood, bend the nerves, unite the spirits, quicken the senses, strengthen the muscles, and thereby rouse up, provoke, excite, and enable a man to the vigorous accomplishment of the feat of amorous dalliance. I have no need of those, quoth Panurge, God be thanked, and you, my good master. However, I pray you, take no exception or offence at these my words; for what I have said was not out of any ill will I did bear to you, the Lord, he knows.

Thirdly, The ardor of lechery is very much subdued and check'd by frequent labor and continual toiling. For by painful exercises and laborious working, so great a dissolution is brought upon the whole body, that the blood, which runneth alongst the channels of the veins thereof, for the nourishment and alimentation of each of its members, hath neither time, leisure, nor power to afford the seminal resudation, or superfluity of the third concoction, which nature most carefully reserves for the conservation of the individual, whose preservation she more heedfully regardeth than the propagating of the species, and the multiplication of human kind.

Whence it is, that Diana is said to be chaste, because she is never idle, but always busied about her hunting. For the same reason was a camp, or leaguer, of old called *Castrum*, as if they would have said *Castum;* because the soldiers, wrestlers, runners, throwers of the bar, and other such like athletic champions, as are usually seen in a military circumvallation, do incessantly travail and turmoil, and are in perpetual stir and agitation. To this purpose Hippocrates also writeth in his book, *De Aere, Aqua, et Locis,* That in his time there was a people in Scythia, as impotent as eunuchs in the discharge of a venerean exploit; because that without any cessation, pause, or respite, they were never from off horseback, or otherwise assiduously employed in some troublesome and molesting drudgery.

On the other part, in opposition and repugnancy hereto, the philosophers say, That idleness is the mother of luxury. When it was asked Ovid, Why Aegisthus became an adulterer? he made no other answer but this, Because he was idle. Who were able to rid the world of loitering and laziness might easily frustrate and disappoint Cupid of all his designs, aims, engines, and devices, and so disable and appal him that his bow, quiver, and darts should from thenceforth be a mere needless load and burthen to him, for that it could not then lie in his power to strike, or wound any of either sex, with all the arms he had. He is not, I believe, so expert an archer, as that he can hit the cranes flying in the air, or yet the young stags skipping through the thickets, as the Parthians knew well how to do, that is to say, people moiling, stirring, and hurrying up and down, restless, and without repose. He must have those hushed, still, quiet, lying at a stay, lither, and full of ease, whom he is able to pierce with all his arrows. In confirmation hereof, Theophrastus being asked on a time, What kind of beast or thing he judged a toyish, wanton love to be? he made answer, That it was a passion of idle and sluggish spirits. From which pretty description of ticking love-tricks, that of Diogenes's hatching was not very discrepant, when he defined lechery, The occupation of folks destitute of all other occupation. For this cause the Sicyonian sculptor Canachus, being desirous to give us to understand that sloth, drowsiness, negligence, and laziness were the prime guardians and governesses of ribaldry, made the statue of Venus, not standing, as other stonecutters had used to do, but sitting.

Fourthly, the tickling pricks of incontinency, are blunted by an eager study; for from thence proceedeth an incredible resolution of the spirits, that oftentimes there do not remain so many behind as may suffice to push and thrust forwards the generative resudation to the places thereto appropriated, and there withal inflate the cavernous nerve, whose office is to ejaculate the moisture for the propagation of human progeny. Lest you should think it is not so, be pleased but to contemplate a little the form, fashion, and carriage of a man exceeding earnestly set upon some learned meditation, and deeply plunged therein, and you shall see how all the arteries of his brains are stretched forth, and bent like the string of a cross-bow, the more promptly, dexterously, and copiously to suppeditate, furnish and supply him with store of spirits, sufficient to replenish and fill up the ventricles, seats, tunnels, mansions, receptacles, and cellules of common sense,— of the imagination, apprehension, and fancy,—of the ratiocination, arguing, and resolution,—as likewise of the memory, recordation, and remembrance; and with great alacrity, nimbleness, and agility to run, pass, and course from the one to the other, through those pipes, windings, and conduits, which to skilful anatomists are perceivable at the end of the wonderful net, where all the arteries close in a terminating point, which arteries, taking their rise and origin from the left capsule of the heart, bring through several circuits, ambages, and anfractuosities, the vital spirits, to subtilize and refine them to the aetherial purity of animal spirits . . .

I remember to have read, that Cupid on a time being asked of his mother Venus, why he did not assault and set upon the Muses, his answer was, That he found them so fair, so sweet, so fine, so neat, so wise, so learned, so modest, so discreet, so courteous, so virtuous, and so continually busied and employed, that approaching near unto them he unbent his bow, shut his quiver, and extinguished his torch, through mere shame, and fear that by mischance he might do them some hurt or prejudice . . . Under this article may be comprised what Hippocrates wrote in the afore-cited treatise concerning the Scythians; as also that in a book of his, entitled, Of Breeding and Production, where he hath affirmed all such men to be unfit for generation, as have their parotid arteries cut—whose situation is beside the ears —for the reason given already, when I was speaking of the resolution of the spirits, and of that spiritual blood whereof the arteries are the sole and proper receptacles; and that likewise he doth maintain a large portion of parastatic liquor to issue and descend from the brains and backbone.

Fifthly, by the too frequent reiteration of the act of venery. There did I wait for you, quoth Panurge, and shall willingly apply it to myself, whilst any one that pleaseth may, for me, make use of any of the four preceding. That is the very same thing, quoth Friar John, which Father Scyllino, Prior of Saint Victor at Marseilles, calleth by the name of maceration, and taming of the flesh. I am of the same opinion,—and so was the hermit of Saint Radegonde, a little above Chinon: for, quoth he, the hermits of Thebaide can no way more aptly or expediently macerate and bring down the pride of their bodies, daunt and mortify their lecherous sensuality, or depress and overcome the stubbornness and rebellion of the flesh, than by duffling and fanfreluching it five and twenty or thirty times a day.

Aphrodisiac Secrets

Since sexual activity was primarily associated with procreation, and procreation was the basis of a society's continued existence, rites and mystic knowledge involving sexual matters and methods of stimulating amatory tendencies were vested in small, specialized, secretive agencies, notably priests and sorcerers. This was the situation particularly in ancient Egypt, Greece, and Rome.

Aphrodisiacs For Sale

In ancient Rome, love concoctions of all kinds were sold publicly. Poets and Imperial officials, travelers and roués, idle matrons and hardened soldiers resorted to such aphrodisiac support without hesitation, without self-consciousness.

Among the ingredients of such preparations were the astroit or star-fish, the remora or sucking-fish, dried human marrow, even *sanguis menstruus* and *semen virile*. While these concoctions were being prepared, earnest invocations were offered to the Infernal Deities.

Aphrodisiac Stimulation

It should be noted that such stimulus may be induced visually by lascivious photographs, by the reading of libidinous books, by viewing paintings and sculpture of an amatory nature, as in the case, for instance, of the obscene frescoes and wall paintings that have survived in Pompeian excavations, or the Caves of Ajanta in Hyderabad, India, some of them dating back to the second century B.C. and containing equally lascivious and erotic frescoes.

Aphrodisiac Wine

An Italian recipe that has a presumptive amatory effect contains, in addition to wine, ginger, cinnamon, rhubarb, and vanilla.

Another wine recipe consists of, Madeira wine, two pieces of sugar, four drops of curaçao.

Aphrodisin

A proprietary preparation compounded of the aphrodisiac yohimbine, together with aronacein, extract of miura puama, and other ingredients.

Aphrodite

According to the ancient Greek poet Hesiod, in his *Theogony,* which describes the origins of the divinities, Aphrodite, goddess of love, sprang from the severed membrum of Uranus, the sky god. Hence Aphrodite was considered under two forms. As Aphrodite Urania, she was the goddess of pure, wedded love. As Aphrodite Pandemos, she was the goddess of free love that was open to purchase.

Aphrodite as Patroness

Aphrodite, the goddess of love, presided over every sexual manifestation. As Aphrodite Hetaira she was the patron goddess of the female amatory companions of the Greeks. Under the name of Aphrodite Porne she was the divine protectress of prostitutes and of a variety of sexual activities.

In Sparta, she was also known as Aphrodite Peribaso, Aphrodite the Streetwalker. As Aphrodite Trymalitis, she symbolized the ultimate sexual consummation.

Aphrodite Kallipygos

Aphrodite, the Greek goddess of love, was represented, in poetry and sculpture, as endowed with such alluring charms, such sexual enticements, as to infatuate even the wise men, as Homer adds. Throughout Greece, in temples dedicated to the goddess, her kallipygian beauty was stressed as a factor in her worship.

Apium Petroselinum

This is the common parsley. Called in the Middle Ages petersilie. Used in garnishing food. Also traditionally considered an effective aid in aphrodisiac directions.

Apothecary Burton

In the seventeenth century an English apothecary named Burton opened in the town of Colchester a factory where he produced aphrodisiac confections derived from sea holly roots.

Apple

In ancient Greece and in Rome the apple had a symbolical erotic connotation. Lovers or would-be lovers exchanged apples as presents, or threw them to each other.

Mythologically, a certain Acontius was in love with Cydippe. As the love was reciprocated, he wrote 'I swear by Artemis that I will wed Acontius' on an apple. Cydippe read the words aloud, and although she threw the apple away, she finally accepted Acontius.

Powdered white thorn apples, black pepper, honey, long pepper, compounded into an ointment, is recommended, in Hindu sexology, as an irresistible means of achieving sexual mastery.

In mediaeval Germany it was a popular belief that an apple steeped in the perspiration of the loved woman would excite amorous advances.

Apricot Brandy

Considered an aphrodisiac liqueur. The possible reason is that it is pleasant in itself and is conducive to a relaxed condition of well-being. Traditionally, wines and liqueurs, in moderation, as well as wholesome foods, all tend to promote erotic inclinations.

Apuleius

A Roman orator and philosopher who flourished in the second century A.D. He also wrote a strange romantic novel entitled *The Golden Ass* or *Metamorphoses*. It contains exciting adventures, magic episodes, unique festivals and rites, and a great deal of matter relating to sexual activities, aphrodisiacs, and amatory displays.

Virtually, this romantic novel has the force of a verbal aphrodisiac. It belongs in the same amatory category as the *Decameron* and Honoré de Balzac's *Contes Drôlatiques*.

Apuleius on Philtres

Apuleius, a Roman philosopher and novelist who flourished in the second century A.D., wrote on magic and occult practices. Of philtres he says,

They dig up all kinds of philtres from everywhere, antidotes, pills, roots, herbs, hippomanes.

See *PHILTRES*

Aquamarine

An engraved aquamarine was used among Arabs as a love charm to secure conjugal fidelity.

Periapts, talismans, and various types of charms all play a prominent part, in both European and Oriental erotology, as at least putative amatory stimulants.

Arabian Nights

In the story of Ala-al Din abu-al, a druggist prepares a love potion containing cubebs,

After hearing Sham-al Din's story, the druggist betook himself to a hashish seller, of whom he bought two ounces of concentrated Roumi opium and equal parts of Chinese cubebs, cinnamon, cloves, cardamoms, ginger, white pepper, and mountain shiek—an aphrodisiac lizard; and pounding them all together boiled them in sweet olive oil; after which he added three ounces of male frankincense in fragments and a cupful of coriander seed, and macerating the whole made it into an electuary with Roumi bee-honey. Then he put the confection in the bowl and carried it to the merchant, saying, 'Take of my electuary with a spoon after supping, and wash it down with a sherbet made of rose conserve; but first sup off mutton and house pigeon plentifully seasoned and hotly spiced.'

Sir Richard Burton's commentaries on the *Arabian Nights* dwell at great length on Oriental views and attitudes toward love, amatory techniques, aphrodisiacs, and the entire erotic field.

Arab Ideal

Like the ancient Greeks, the Arabs have their own ethnic

standards of female beauty, the cumulative presence of which, in any particular woman, would inspire the most extreme amatory expression.

This ideal includes a body white as ivory, teeth like rice in whiteness and glow, the gait and step of a young spirited mare or a doe. This ideal woman's hair is black, and hangs in thick tresses. Her lashes are curved, her breasts firm, her hips wide.

In figure she should stand upright, like a palm tree that grows skyward in the oasis. With her narrow waist, and perfumed with myrrh, and adorned with tinkling jewelry, she can allure any man by her seductive presence without the aid of any other contrived aphrodisiacs.

Arabs

Of all peoples, the Arabs have made almost a science of erotic writing. Their literature abounds in studies and manuals that discuss the physiology of love, amorous skills, aphrodisiacs and anaphrodisiacs, and in a wider sense the entire range of sexual relationships, both normal and abnormal.

Arab Tales

The Perfumed Garden, one of the major erotic manuals originally intended for Moslem use, is full of anecdotes illustrating some particular phase of amatory activity—pervaded, in most cases, by expressions of devoutness, sanctity, poetic imagery, and verse.

In this respect, the book is highly reminiscent of the *Arabian Nights,* and in some degree the forerunner of Boccaccio and Rabelais.

See *PERFUMED GARDEN.*

Arab Ways

E. W. Lane, nineteenth century traveler and authority on Egypt, emphasizes the widespread indulgence in sexual activity in Arab countries. Sexual interest takes precedence over all other human affairs. But underlying such amatory expression lies a religious motif, an explicit injunction governing erotic mores as a sacred function and a devout duty.

Sexual desires, then, according to Arab concepts, should not be discouraged, but rather actively stimulated. Hence, in line with such positive prescriptions, the continuous search for foods, drugs such as opium and hashish, and other aphrodisiac devices and aids in the prolongation and promotion of sexual powers.

Arab Women

Nefzawi, in *The Perfumed Garden,* breaks out into this exultant eulogy of women,

Then the Almighty has plunged women into a sea of splendors, of voluptuousness, and of delights, and covered her with precious vestments, with brilliant girdles and provoking smiles.

Nefzawi, describing the provocative features of woman, adds,

He has also gifted her with eyes that inspire love, and with eyelashes like polished blades.

See *PERFUMED GARDEN.*

Aristophanes

A Greek comedy writer of the fourth century B.C. In one of his plays, *Lysistrata,* he refers to the seductive sexual attraction inspired by women clad in 'diaphanous garments of yellow silk and long flowing gowns, decked out with flowers, and shod with dainty little slippers.'

'Those yellow tunics,' adds one of the female characters, 'those scents and slippers, those cosmetics and transparent robes are the very sheet-anchors of women's salvation.'

Aristotelian Recipe

In the *Golden Cabinet of Secrets,* a work attributed erroneously to Aristotle, there is a recipe for making a love powder.

Take elecampane, the seeds or flowers, vervain, and the berries of mistletoe. Beat them, after being well dried in an oven, into a powder, and give it to the party you design upon in a glass of wine and it will work wonderful effect to your advantage.

Aristotle

The entire corpus of Aristotelian writings is so vast that in many cases, through the centuries, various treatises have been attributed to Aristotelian authorship. Among such works are *Problems,* that discuss medical, physical, and biological matters.

One section is devoted to sexual questions. Questions are first propounded and then answered in sequence. Among these questions are the following,

Why do men more rapidly copulate when fasting?

Why do young men, when they first begin to copulate, after the act, hate those with whom they copulate?

Is it because a great mutation is effected?

Why do those who ride on horseback continually become more libidinous?

Why are men less able to copulate in the water?

Why are those lascivious from whose eyelids the hairs fall off?

Why are men in winter, but women in summer, more impelled to venery?

Why are those that are melancholy addicted to venery?

Is it because they abound with hot air?

Why are birds, and men that are hairy, lascivious?

Is it because they possess more moisture?

Why, when man engages in venery, are his eyes especially weakened?

Armagnac

Henry IV of France, before confronting his numerous mistresses, regularly fortified himself with a tiny glass of armagnac.

Wines and liqueurs have long been held to promote sexual activities.

34

Arnaud De Villeneuve

A thirteenth century polymath who asserted that the mere possession of an article fashioned from the wood of agnus castus produced an anti-aphrodisiac effect.

See *AGNUS CASTUS*

Aromatic Baths

Among the Romans, especially in the luxurious Imperial age, aromatic baths constituted a regular prelude and instigation for amatory practice. Similarly, perfumed unguents were used by the attendants who massaged the bodies of the bathers.

The impact of perfume on amatory expression has long been known to the Oriental sexologists, especially the Arabs, whose manuals are packed with hints and advice on the use of such amatory aids.

The olfactory sense intervenes with some people to awaken venereal desire. The olfactory nerves and the erotic challenge are closely linked. This association is illustrated in a rare piece written by Lafcadio Hearn on *odor feminae*.

Arnobius

In connection with the obscene goddess Venus Pertunda, Arnobius, one of the Fathers of the Church who belongs to the fourth century A.D., describes the significance of the name Pertunda,

Pertunda in cubiculis praesto est virginalem scrobem effodientibus maritis.

Arris

A Hindu technique for dominating women sexually is to take pieces of arris root, mixed with mango oil. Place in a hole in the trunk of the sisu tree, and so leave for six months. At the end of that time an ointment is prepared that may effectively be applied to the lingam.

Arsinoe

The daughter of the King of Cyprus. Rejected the love

of Arceophon, who committed suicide. As a punishment, Aphrodite, goddess of love, turned the frigid Arsinoë into stone.

Such a myth, to the ancients, acted as a warning, and exemplified the all-powerful force of love that is cosmically all-pervasive.

Artemisia

This genus of aromatic plants includes wormwood and mugwort. Used as a condiment in amatory cooking.

Artichoke

A bristly plant whose edible parts are the fleshy bases of the leaves. Considered a powerful aphrodisiac, especially in France. Street vendors in Paris had a special cry,

Artichokes! Artichokes!
Heats the body and the spirit.
Heats the genitals.
Catherine de Medici was fond of artichokes.

Consumption of artichokes may directly produce euphoria; indirectly, this sense of pleasant relaxation is highly conducive to amatory exercise.

Ashmole

Elias Ashmole, a seventeenth century English alchemist, who offered amorous advice in the following verses,

I asked philosophy how I should
Have of her the thing I would;
She answered me when I was able
To make the water malleable;
Or else the way if I could find
To measure out a yard of wind,
Then shalt thou have thine own desire,
When thou can'st weigh an ounce of fire,
Unless that thou can'st do these three,
Content thyself, thou gets not me.

36

Asoka

In Hindu sexology, the asoka plant, the lotus, and jasmine provoke venery.

The lotus itself is associated with the Lotus-Woman, the Hindu feminine ideal.

Asparagus

A daily dish of asparagus, first boiled then fried in fat, with egg yolks and a sprinkling of condiments, will, according to an Arab manual, produce considerable erotic effects.

Ass

In Greek mythology, the ass was the symbol of sexual potency. This animal was associated with satyrs and sileni, creatures who in their characteristics resembled satyrs.

See *SATYRS*.

On one occasion, at a Dionysiac festival, Priapus, personification of the sexual impulse, was about to consummate his sexual desire for the nymph Lotis. The braying of an ass, however, interrupted the performance. Since then, the ass became a sacrificial victim of Priapus.

Athenaeus

Athenaeus of Naucratis in Egypt was a Greek writer of the second century A.D. He is the author of a *Banquet of the Philosophers*, extant now in fifteen books that are filled with quotations, anecdotes, information on religion and literature, morals and medicine, and particularly foods and items of amatory interest.

Aubergine

An aubergine, split in half, a paste made of flour, water, in which bois bandé has been boiled, together with peppercorns, chives, pimentos, vanilla beans. This concoction was used in the West Indies as a genital excitant.

See *BOIS BANDÉ*.

Audile Aphrodisiac

The voice, in inflection or tone or volume or by some other peculiarity of the individual, can be a deeply stirring incitement. Thus it is possible to fall in love with a voice, both fictionally and in reality.

In a similar direction, music may have effects of the same nature. A great many of Wagner's operatic pieces, for instance, have, for many listeners, a sexually rousing appeal.

Franz Liszt's Hungarian Rhapsody, too, in its swelling, tumultuous and orgiastic crescendo movements, may produce similar excitation.

Avena Sativa

Considered at one time as an effective aphrodisiac.

A difficulty that arises frequently is the rarity of the ingredient or plant or its inaccessibility or its attendant hazards.

Avicenna

Famous thirteenth century Arab philosopher and physician. His Arab name is Abu Ali al-Hussain ibn Sina. A noted libertine as well, he discusses in his writings erotic questions, sexual procedures, and aphrodisiacs.

B

Bacchae

The Bacchae, a tragedy by the Greek dramatist Euripides, is one of the primary sources for the study of the ancient Bacchic cult.

See *BACCHUS.*

Bacchus

Ancient divinity of wine and fertility. Variously associated with Dionysus, whose cult was marked by orgiastic revelries. Festivals involved procreative rites and phallic worship.

In all erotic literature, both factual and imaginative, wine, food, and amatory expression go hand in hand.

An illustration of this concept appears in Omar Khayyam's *Rubaiyat,*

A loaf of bread, a jug of wine, and thou.

Bah-Nameh

Book of Delight. A Turkish collection of amorous tales by Abdul Hagg Effendi. Contains allusions to aphrodisiacs.

Baiae

An ancient Roman pleasure resort, somewhat like contemporary Nice. It was the focal point of all kinds of erotic experiments, unbridled debauchery, amorous intrigues and excitations, sexual encounters and aberrations.

The philosopher and tutor to the Emperor Nero, Seneca, inveighs against the abandoned and lascivious atmosphere of the resort. It is, he declares in one of his Letters, characterized by all-night revelry, drunkenness on the beach, banquets in boats, and uninhibited orgies and festivities. All this, apart from the hot sulphur springs that were the ostensible object of visitors who sought curative treatments, tended to extreme aphrodisiac diversions.

Bamboo Shoots
They are believed to produce aphrodisiac reactions. Popular in the Orient, particularly in China, in culinary practice.

Bananas
Considered to have stimulating aphrodisiac properties.

In all such cases, no single use of the food will be effective. What is true is that the continued consumption of, say, bananas, will be an aid in amatory directions.

Banquets
The lavish feasts that are historically associated with particular nations, notably the Romans, and those that are attached to the names of Nebuchadnezzar, Sardanapalus, and Alexander the Great, the similar lavish entertainments of the courts of medieval Italy and the royal families of France were all directed, in the ultimate sense, toward sexual excesses, so that the Bacchic and gastronomic stimuli were mere preliminaries of erotic culminations.

The Latin apothegm applies to such luxurious entertainments no less than to the intimate *petit souper,*

Sine Baccho et Cerere frigescit Venus, Without wine and food love grows cold.

Barbel
This fish, well prepared, helps to restore virility. The tradition is old, but in line with the general view of the stimulating properties of fish.

Basil
An aromatic plant used in food as a condiment. Has reputedly aphrodisaic qualities.

In Italy, basil was used by girls as a love charm.

According to an early nineteenth century physician, basil "helps the deficiency of Venus."

Bath

In the degenerate and luxurious Roman Imperial Age, baths that both men and women used in common were in vogue. The heterosexual proximities stimulated at the same time amorous advances. In addition, attendants at these baths, that had special hot, cold, and steam rooms, were regularly of the opposite sexes. Attendants and bathers consequently were exposed to sexual provocations during the entire procedure.

In the Middle Ages, it was customary for girls to serve in similar capacities as attendants to cavaliers and knights during their bathing. This was the case particularly in Germany, where the public baths became virtual brothels.

In Japan, the custom is still contemporary.

Bathory

In the seventeenth century Countess Elizabeth Bathory was a notorious Hungarian, In her attempts to achieve rejuvenation, she bathed in the blood of eighty peasant girls who had been strangled to death. Caught in the act, she was condemned to life imprisonment.

Baudelaire

Charles Baudelaire, the nineteenth century French poet, in his *Les Paradis Artificiels,* describes the erotic fantasies conjured up in his mind by the use of hashish.

Baudelaire on Hashish

Charles Baudelaire, in his *Les Paradis Artificiels,* analyzes the effects of hashish and opium. He makes a comprehensive survey of the drugs, in a historical and botanical sense. A discussion on the effects follows. The morality implicit in the administration of the drugs comes in for lengthy comment, Baudelaire stressing the Man-God as a release from himself and his chthonic chains. Baudelaire now examines Thomas de Quincey's *Confessions of an English Opium-Eater* (de Quincey had just died at this time), with further notations on the pleasures of the drug and also the torments it produces.

The entire study, rich in imagery and expressed with great clarity and sensitivity, should be read in its entirety.

See *BAUDELAIRE*.

See *HASHISH*.

Beans

St. Jerome forbade nuns to partake of beans, because *in partibus genitalibus titillationes producunt.*

In the Middle Ages, special anaphrodisiac foods, plants, and preparations were administered to monks to diminish or eliminate all carnal tendencies.

Beefsteak

Havelock Ellis, the sexologist, regards the beefsteak as "Probably as powerful a sexual stimulant as any food."

Beer

In England, popular belief attributes to beer a coital stimulus. Medical authority recommends that beer be taken along with food.

Beets

White beets are mentioned by Pliny the Elder, the Roman encyclopedist, as helpful in promoting amorous capacity.

In general, beets, carrots, and turnips are all of aphrodisiac value in erotic dietary.

Belief in Flagellation

For long centuries flagellant treatment was considered of ultimate effectiveness. As a means of restoring vigor to the generative organs, flagellation was recommended by ancient physicians as an effectual remedy, in accordance with the Hippocratic principle of *ubi stimulus, ibi affluxus.*

Seneca, the Roman Stoic philosopher, considered flagellation as a remedy for the quartan ague. Jerome Mercurialis describes flagellation as an aid in increasing the weight of thin and meagre persons. Galen, the famous Greek authority whose reputation lasted well into the Middle Ages, adds that it was used by slave merchants as a means of making the slaves plump and more appealing for sale.

Richter, in his *Opuscula Medica,* refers to the treatment as a sexual stimulus,

ex stimulantium fonte, cardiaca, aphrodisiaca, diaphoretica, diuretica, aliaque non infimi ordinis medicamenta peti.

In the seventeenth century, Meibomius extensively advocated this remedy. He wrote a monograph on the subject, entitled *De Flagrorum Usu in Re Venerea.*

A couplet, introducing the volume, runs as follows in the English translation,

> Lo! Cruel stripes the sweets of love insure,
> And painful pleasures pleasing pains procure.

Millingen, in his *Curiosities of Medical Experience,* similarly declares that the effect of flagellation may be readily referred to the powerful sympathy which exists between the nerves of the lower part of the spinal marrow and other organs. Artificial excitement appears in some degree natural; it is observed in several animals, especially in the feline race. Even snails plunge into each other a bony, prickly spur, that arises from their throats, and which, like the sting of the wasp, breaks off, and is left in the wound.

The Abbé Boileau, in his *Histoire des Flagellants,* has this to say,

> Necesse est cum musculi lumbares virgis aut
> flagellis diverberantur, spiritus vitales

revelli, adeoque salaces motus ob viciniam partium genita-
lium et testium excitari, qui venereis illecebris cerebrum
mentemque fascinant ac virtutem castitatis ad extremas
angustias redigunt.

According to Pliny the Elder, the Roman encyclopedist,
Cornelius Gallus, friend of the Roman poet Vergil, had
to resort to the scourge in order to achieve amatory consummations.

Another instance refers to a notorious Italian libertine,
who used a whip steeped in vinegar,

> Plus on le fouettait, plus il
> y trouvait des délices, la

douleur et la volupté marchant, dans cet homme,
d'um pas égal.

A French epitaph alludes to a similar circumstance,

> Je suis mort de l'amour entrepris
> Entre les jambes d'une dame,
> Bien heureux d'avoir rendu l'âme,
> Au même lieu où je l'ai pris.

It has also been conjectured that Abelard employed this
means. In writing to Héloise, he declares,

> Verbera quandoque dabat amor non furor,
> gratia non ira, quae omnium unguentorum
> suavitatem transcenderent.
> Stripes which, whenever inflicted by love,
> not by fury but affection, transcended,
> in their sweetness, every unguent.

Again he rebukes himself,

> Thou knowest to what shameful excesses my
> unbridled lust had delivered up our bodies,
> so that no sense of decency, no reverence
> for God, could, even in the season of our
> Lord's passion, or during any other holy
> festival, drag me forth from out that
> cesspool of filthy mire; but that even

with threats and scourges I often compelled
thee who wast, by nature, a weaker vessel,
to comply, notwithstanding thy unwillingness
and remonstrances.

The same practices are recorded in the case of Tamerlane,
the Asiatic conqueror, who was also a monorchis.

A certain Abbé Chuppe d'Auteroche, who died late in
the eighteenth century, asserted that in Russia, in the vapor
baths, stripes were administered to the frequenters as a
stimulus to the venereal appetite.

Jean Jacques Rousseau was likewise susceptible to flagellation,

J'avais trouvé dans la douleur, dans la honte même, un
mélange de sensualité qui m'avait laissé plus de désir que de
crainte de l'éprouver derechef.

Belladonna

A dangerous, poisonous drug, extracted from the root and
leaves of the Deadly Nightshade. The name stems from the
fact that Italian beauties made a cosmetic from the juice
of the plant. The juice of the berry was used for the eyes,
to enlarge the pupils. In the Middle Ages belladonna formed
an ingredient in the philtres and unguents prepared by
witches, but it has no aphrodisiac value.

Beverages

Ordinary coffee and tea, drunk to excess, may reputedly
produce anaphrodisiac results.

Bhang

A Sanskrit term meaning *hemp*.

In India, the leaves and seeds of hemp are chewed as a
means of increasing sexual capacity. Frequently the seeds of
hemp are mixed with musk, sugar, and ambergris, to which
aphrodisiac virtues are ascribed.

The seed capsules and leaves are often used to make an
infusion, which is drunk as a liquor.

45

Bhuya-Kokali

A Hindu plant, botanically termed Solanum Jacquini, that is suggested by the Hindu *Ananga-Ranga,* the erotic guide, as a factor in inducing aphrodisiac power. The juice of the plant is dried in the sun and then mixed with honey, ghee or clarified butter, and candied sugar.

Biblical Enticements

There is mention in the Bible of amatory seductiveness,
Moreover the Lord saith, Because the daughters of Zion are haughty, and walk with stretched forth necks and wanton eyes, walking and mincing as they go, and making a tinkling with their feet.
Isaiah 3.16.

Biblical Orgies

Among the ancient Semites sexual sensuality was so dominant that restraints were imposed by legal and religious prohibitions. Sometimes such restrictions were completely abrogated and disdained, the consequences being the wildest and most uninhibited orgies. An instance of such license occurs in the episode of the Golden Calf: Exodus 32. 6,19.

Biblical Terms

The genitalia and other sexual areas and functions are regularly expressed in Biblical literature in euphemistic or allusive terms. The *membrum virile* becomes the flesh. The genitalia are variantly referred to as nakedness, feet, shames, loin, and thigh.
Coitus is uniformly equated with lying.

Bird Nest Soup

An extremely aphrodisiac Chinese preparation.
The nests are those of the sea swallow, made from sea weed that is edible. The leaves are stuck together by fish spawn, which abounds in phosphorus. The soup, in addition, is highly spiced.

Birthwort
A shrub in use among the Romans as an aphrodisiac. It was also so used in medieval times.

Bitter Sweet
A herb that was formerly reputed to have some erotic value.
This, however, is most probably a traditional and untested view.

Bone
A Hindu erotic text suggests the stimulating and alluring effect of bone of peacock or hyena, covered with gold, and tied to the right hand.

Book of Age-Rejuvenation in the Power of Concupiscence
An Arab amatory manual by Ahmad bin Sulayman. Deals with many phases of sexology, and makes specific recommendations along erotic lines.

Blood
Human blood has been thought to be anti-aphrodisiac and has been so used. Faustina, the wife of the Emperor Antoninus Pius, fell in love with a gladiator. The magicians whom the Emperor consulted advised that she drink her lover's blood, the effect being that she would conceive a permanent hatred for the gladiator. She did so, and the result was completely efficacious.

Boccaccio (Giovanni) On Love (1313-1375)
Beauty is a fatal gift for those who want to live virtuously.
In love, however, women are brave. How many clamber over rooftops of houses and palaces, and are still doing it, when their lovers await them! How many hide their admirers in chests or closets, before their husbands' very eyes! How many, lying next to him, have had them come even into their beds! How many sneak at night through lines of

armed troops, or hasten across the sea, through cemeteries, to the one who beguiled them!

Since man is more constant, and yet cannot control himself—I will not just say to meet the willing beauty, but even to desire the one who pleases his senses—he will not only desire her, but do everything to possess her. And as this happens to him not just once a month but a thousand times a day, how can we exepect that woman, who by nature is easily persuaded, should resist the temptation, the flattery, the gifts and a thousand other tricks, an astute admirer resorts to?

If you pursue the study of beautiful women, they will teach you that those who play with love, trifle away their chance to become happy through it.

Small gifts, flowers and finery of insignificant value will always serve well. But a lady who accepts gold and precious things from her admirer does not really love him in her heart; she merely covets his riches, and when this source is dried up, she will forsake him. Avoid such a beauty like a snake that menaces your life, and consider it as the surest sign of the genuineness or falsity of her feelings, whether she rejects or accepts your precious gifts.

Bois Bandé

Tightening wood. A concoction administered in the West Indies by women. It has the reputed virtue of an aphrodisiac.

The ingredients contain the bark of a tree which itself contains bucine and a little strychnine. The preparation, an anthropologist declares, may produce poisoning.

Book of Exposition

This is an Arabic erotic work entitled Kitab al—Izah fi'llm al—Nikah b-it—w-al—Kamal. Attributed, but not definitively, to a certain Jalal ad-din as—Siyuti.

Although it deals in abundant and frank details with the most intimate erotic procedures, its tone, like that of

48

similar Oriental manuals, is free from contrived obscenity or ribaldry. There is, in fact, implicit throughout, an attitude of reverence for the universal cosmic force that divinely governs all such human conditions. This tone is also evident in Nefzawi's *The Perfumed Garden.*

See *PERFUMED GARDEN.*

Borax

According to seventeenth century belief, refined borax excites powerful desire. Nicolas Venette, a Frenchman, recommends it as a substance that readily pervades all parts of the body. It should, however, be used in moderation.

See *VENETTE.*

Bourbons

The French dynasty of the Bourbons, whose ascendency began with Henry IV early in the seventeenth century and spread over France, Spain, and Sicily, were notorious for their amatory skills and their ingenuities in erotic foods and drinks.

Bracelet Device

Pliny the Elder states that, to increase sexual potency, the right testis of an ass should be worn in a bracelet. Such advice coincides with popular Oriental belief in the efficacy, for amatory purposes, of various types of charms and talismans.

Brain

The brain of calf, sheep, and pig, young and served fresh, is reputedly erotic in its effects. As a side dish in Mediterranean countries, brains are a special delicacy when properly prepared.

Breton Custom

Aphrodisiac techniques intended to cure sterility have been known to women for millennia. In India even in contemporary times women make offerings to certain trees, in the hope that the deity associated with the tree will make a beneficent response.

Breton customs, lingering through the centuries in this almost isolated area of France, are similarly associated with phallic rites, directed toward the same end.

In one town, a phallic statue was the focal point to which sterile women advanced. Taking some of the dust around the effigy, they swallowed it, in the same hope that possessed the Hindu women.

Brillat-Savarin
A famous French gourmet of the early nineteenth century. Author of *Physiology of Taste*. Of truffles, he says,
It makes women more amiable and men more amorous.
See *TRUFFLES*.

Broad Bean Soup
In Italy, often taken as an assumed aphrodisiac. Beans in general have long been believed to possess amatory virtue.

Brothels
In the eighteenth century, in England, on account of the spreading knowledge that food and drink exerted definite influence on amatory expression, public brothels were at the same time eating houses.

Brya
According to Pliny the Elder, the Roman encyclopedist, the ashes of the plant called in Latin *brya*, mixed with the urine of an ox, produced impotence.

Bufotenin
A dangerous drug that is chemically related to mescaline. See *MESCALINE*.

The drug is obtained from the skin of a poisonous tropical toad. The substance bufotoxin is the chief extract of the toad's venom. This alkaloid is also present in the seeds of a mimosa plant that is related to the *leguminosae* family.

50

The natives of some South American tribes use this drug as an aphrodisiac in the form of a snuff called *cohoba*. Bufotenin is capable of producing severe hallucinations of a psycho-erotic nature. Its use is highly dangerous and in any case requires the supervision and control of a physician or psychiatrist.

Burgundy

In moderation, considered a wholesome aphrodisiac.

This is in line with traditional belief in the amatory encouragements produced by wines and liqueurs taken in moderation.

Burton

In his *Anatomy of Melancholy*, Robert Burton, the seventeenth century chronicler, has this to say of aphrodisiacs,

The last battering engines are philtres, amulets, charms, images and such unlawful means. If they cannot prevail of themselves by the help of bawds, panders, and their adherents, they will fly for succor to the devil himself. I know there be those that denye the devil can do any such thing, and that there is no other fascination than that which comes by the eyes. It was given out, of old, that a Thessalian wench had bewitched King Philip to dote on her, and by philtres enforced his love, but when Olympia, his queen, saw the maid of an excellent beauty well brought up and qualified, these, quoth she, were the philtres which enveagled King Philip.

Burton goes on,

One accent from thy lips the blood more warmes, Than all their philtres, exorcisms, and charms.

With this alone, Lucretia brags, in Aretine, she could do more than all philosophers, astrologers, alchymists, necromancers, witches, and the rest of the crew. As for herbs and philtres, I could never skill of them,

The sole philtre I ever used was kissing and embracing,

by which alone I made men rave like beasts, stupefied and compelled them to worship me like an idol.

In the text of Petrus Aretinus, the medieval scholar, the Latin runs as follows,

Verum omni ista scientia numquam potui movere cor hominis sola vero saliva mea (id est amplexu et basiis) iniungens, tam furiose furere, tam bestialiter obstupefieri plurimos coegi ut instar idoli me Amoresque meos adorarint.

Buttermilk Bath

An anti-aphrodisiac, suggested in Hindu erotological literature as a way for a women to negate amatory challenges, is to bathe in the buttermilk of a she-buffalo. The milk is to be mixed with powders of the gopalika plant, the banupadika plant, and yellow amaranth.

Metropolitan Museum of Art, Kennedy Fund, 1910

PLATE 3—Mars and Venus by Veronese

PLATE 4—The Alchemist (engraving from the original of F. von Mieris)

C

Cabbage
In aphrodisiac preparation, wild cabbage was frequently an ingredient.

This was an old, traditional practice.

Caelius Calcagninus
An obscure mediaeval writer, mentioned by Martin Delrio, who wrote a treatise on amatory procedures entitled *De Amatoria Magia.*

See *DELRIO.*

Cakes
In the Middle Ages, spiced cakes were often baked in a small oven, over the naked body of a woman who wanted to retain the affections of her lover. The witch who carried out the baking technique used this form of sympathetic magic to arouse desire in correspondence with the flaming heat of the oven.

The baked concoction would ultimately be offered to the object of the woman's love. Such cakes were sometimes consumed by both parties, the man and the woman, as a means of strengthening and binding passion.

The practice was common throughout Europe, and not unknown in other countries as well.

Calamint
A fragrant herb that was formerly used in India for erotic practices.

Calves' Brain

Cooked appetizingly, this recipe is recommended as assisting the libido.

See *BRAIN*.

Camel Bone

As an aphrodisiac aid, Indian erotology suggests camel bone, dipped in the juice of the eclipta prostata plant; then burnt. The black pigment produced from the ashes is placed in a box also made of camel bone and then applied with antimony to the eyelashes with the pencil of a camel bone. The effect, it is hinted, will be erotic subjugation.

Camel's Fat

Fat, melted down from the hump of the camel, is suggested in an Oriental manual as an aphrodisiac aid.

Camel's Milk

When mixed with honey and taken for successive days, this drink produces marked potency, according to Arab tradition.

Camphor

A form of camphor known as monobromated camphor is said to have an anaphrodisiac effect.

Canaanites

Among the ancient Canaanites it was considered a divine honor to perform the sexual act. The Hebrew tribes that dwelt in these regions adopted this custom,

And Israel abode in Shittim, and the people began to commit whoredom with the daughters of Moab.

And they called the people unto the sacrifices of their gods; and the people did eat, and bowed down to their gods.

And Israel joined himself unto Baal-peor, and the anger of the Lord was kindled against Israel.

Numbers 25. 1-3.

Cannabis Indica

Indian hemp. A drug that was used for centuries as an aphrodisiac.

This plant grows in Central and Western Asia and the Western Himalayas, in India, Africa, and North America. The resin extracted from the plant is called *cannabinon,* from which *cannabinol* stems, a red oily substance found in the flowering tops of the female plant. Extracted from the plant in pure form, it is known in India as *charas.*

Charas is smoked and eaten. The powdered and sifted form of this resinous substance is *hashish.*

See *HASHISH.*

Another, weaker form, is known as *bhang,* which is used as a beverage.

See *BHANG.*

In Mexico, it is known as *marihuana.* Another form is *ganja,* made from the cut crop of the female plant, it is used for smoking.

Cannabis Indica produces some 150 different preparations of the drug.

For some 5000 years this hemp plant has been known and used from China to Chicago, and throughout the major cities of the world.

In the second millennium B.C. the Chinese were already acquainted with the properties of the hemp plant. In 800 B.C. it was introduced into India, and from that time on it has been cultivated extensively and continuously.

In the seventh century B.C. the Assyrians began to use the drug for its narcotic powers.

In the second century A.D. the ancient Chinese physician Hua Tu administered a narcotic draught to his patients before an operation. The drug was known as *Ma Fu Shuan.* It was used by Dioscorides, the Greek army physician, in the first century A.D. to relieve cases of earache.

The *Arabian Nights* are filled with allusions to hashish. King Omar casts the Princess Alrizah into a deep sleep with some concentrated *bhang*. Again, the thief, Armad Kanakim, drugs the guards with hemp fumes.

Cantharides

A species of beetle known as *mylabris,* also *Lytta Vesicatoria.* Found in Southern Europe. The active principle is a white powder called cantharidine. Cantharides, used externally, may have fatal results. Taken internally, the drug causes death.

Widely used in the eighteenth century as a sexual stimulant. Cooked in biscuits, cakes and pastry, and inserted in candies and chocolates.

An eighteenth century French play refers to the drug, mouches cantharides,

Qui redonnent la force aux amants invalides.

Cantharides was known to Dioscorides, an army physician of the first century A.D., who produced a *Materia Medica,* Galen, a Greek physician of the second century A.D., and the Arab philosopher and physician Avicenna.

Madame de Pompadour used tincture of cantharides to regain the love of Louis XV.

Caperberry

Anciently, the berry of the caper plant was considered a strong aphrodisiac. In the Bible, the term is used synonymously with sexual desire, and the caperberry shall fail, *Ecclesiastes* 12.5.

Capsicum Annuum

From this plant is prepared paprika, Hungarian red pepper. As a condiment in food, paprika is reputed to be strongly aphrodisiac.

Caraway

Caraway has a reputed aphrodisiac virtue. It is frequently mentioned in Oriental love manuals.

Cardamom

A pounded mixture of cardamom spice seeds, ginger, and cinnamon, sprinkled over boiled onions and green peas, is considered, in Arab countries, as an efficacious dish for promoting erotic vigor.

Cardoon

A prickly plant, akin to the artichoke. The fleshy parts of the inner leaves are eaten as an aphrodisiac, especially in France.

Carmina Priapea

A collection of Latin poems, obscene and erotic, that hymn the potency of Priapus.

See *PRIAPUS*.

Carrots

Among Arabs, carrots are eaten as an aphrodisiac.

Stewed in milk sauce, they are recommended as helpful in sexual activity.

In Greece the carrot was popular as a venereal medicine, it was called a *philtron*.

Castor Oil

Once popular among American Indians for erotic purposes.

Castration

Athenaeus, an ancient Greek writer of the third century A.D., author of *Banquet of the Philosophers,* relates that the Medes practised castration among their neighbors in order to excite lust.

Catancy

A plant that the witches of ancient Thessaly, in Greece, used in love philtres.

Caviar

Caviar is generally considered to be a stimulant to sensual inclinations. It is invariably present at dinners and banquets that stress rich, exotic dishes accompanied by appropriate wines, and resulting, for the diners, in a sense of complete euphoria. Such a condition is highly conducive to amatory exercises, as French and other European fiction illustrates so lavishly.

Celery

In eighteenth century France celery soup was a means of whetting the amorous appetite.

It is often included in love recipes.

Celery Cream

This concoction is said to exercise urgency on the *vita sexualis*.

Cestus

The girdle of Venus, that had the power of exciting love.

In Homer's *Iliad*, this girdle is "the charm of love and desire, that subdues all the hearts of the immortal gods and mortal men."

It is mentioned in Ben Jonson's *Volpone*.

Mosca: . . . Why, your gold
    Is such another medicine, it dries up
    All those offensive savors, it transforms
    The most deformed, and restores them lovely,
    As 'twere the strange poetical girdle.

Cevadille

A variant name for spurge.

See *SPURGE*.

Chaldean Device

In ancient Chaldea, magic, religion, and health were inextricably related to each other. So that a physical or mental ailment sought a cure through magical incantations, charms, invocations to the powerful gods.

In the case of amatory functions, it was a belief, fostered by the traditions of Chaldean priests, that vigor and sexual activity could be restored or increased by eating the marrow of the liver of young boys. The belief is identical with that of certain primitive tribes that, both in the African continent and in the Pacific Islands, have sought supreme courage by eating the heart of a vanquished and slain enemy chief.

Chameleon
Milk of chameleon was recommended as an erotic stimulant by Avicenna.

See *AVICENNA*.

Champagne
Long associated, in fiction as well, with erotic situations, amatory relationships, and intimate dining.

In general, wines have traditionally been of significant aid in amatory ventures.

Characteristics of Drugs
Some drugs produce vivid hallucinations, others induce a relaxed condition, or are ataractic in their effect, that is, promote temporary tranquillity, while still others have arousing and exciting impacts.

In many cases, there may be, along with these primary effects, amatory images and stimuli. But the inherent dangers of the drugs transcend any other momentary pleasurable symptoms.

Characteristics of Rosemary
An aromatic shrub indigenous to Southern Europe. The leaves are used medicinally, in perfumery, and in cookery. Also known to the Romans, and reputed as an amatory stimulant.

Characteristics of Women

In his *Les Paradis Artificiels,* Baudelaire declares that man, from the very beginning, has long been bathed in the balmy atmosphere of woman, in the aroma of her hands, her breasts, her knees, her hair, her diaphanous, airy garments.

See *BAUDELAIRE.*

Charms

Among primitive and Oriental races love charms were often associated with the technique known as *sympathetic magic.* A charm was uttered over betel nuts, the nuts were then placed in a box, and the person who opened the box fell in passionate love with the owner.

Or a charm was uttered over the oil used by a woman, or over a lock of her hair. The hoped-for result was similar to an aphrodisiac stimulant.

The ancients, among them the Greeks, felt that the human liver was the seat of all desires. Hence it became a love fetish, an aphrodisiac symbol.

The udder of the hyena, tied on the left arm, enticed the affection of any desired woman.

Cheese

Highly esteemed for its aphrodisiac propensities. Parmesan cheese in particular, in eighteenth century France, was considered highly beneficial in this sense.

Cherries

Stimulating in an amatory sense.

Often included in love cookery.

Chestnuts

Chestnuts, soaked in muscadel, then boiled, along with satyrion, pistachio nuts, pine kernels, cubebs, cinnamon, rocket seed and sugar. Compounded together, these ingredients form a stimulating electuary. This compound was popular as an old English love recipe.

Chick-Peas

Juice of powered onions and purified honey, heated until the onion juice disappears. The residue is then cooled and mixed with water and pounded chick-peas. Taken before bedtime in winter, this beverage is described in an Arab manual as particularly stimulating.

China

Among the most passionate people, according to a Dutch physican, Dr. L. A. Schlegel, are the Chinese. In a book published in 1880 he discusses their amatory mores. Erotic books and engravings, he declares, are largely employed as sexual excitants. Immense quantities of these are to be met with. Nearly all of them, light works, novels, anecdotes are full of expressions of so cynical a nature that it is almost impossible to choose among them.

In the *Tschoen Koeng Ise* (Erotic Poems) history is brought forward for the sole purpose of describing the most scandalous affairs in the vilest language.

The governing authorities allow these books to circulate without any restriction . . . In certain parts of China, they manufacture little articulated and movable puppets, in porcelain or ivory, extremely obscene, known under the name of *Tschoen Koeng Siang.*

The context of these remarks, of course, applies to a period of some eighty years ago.

Chinese

The Chinese, for long centuries, have been familiar with all kinds of aphrodisiacs. A popular compound is cantharides mixed with cloves, cubeb pepper, nutmeg, honey, cinnamon, and saffron.

Chinese Food

Chinese have an intense fondness for the following foods, all of which, it is asserted, contribute to sexual potency when such foods are taken, not intermittently, but as a regular routine over an extended period of time,

Chicken liver, chicken gizzard, tripe, dried shrimp, celery, bamboo shoots, mushrooms, crab, melons, scallops, fried spinach, lettuce, noodles, shark fin, lobsters.

Chin P'ing Mei

A Chinese picaresque erotic novel, written during the sixteenth century. Translated as *The Golden Lotus* by C. Egerton, also translated by Arthur Waley.

This long adventurous novel, somewhat in the manner of the *Metamorphoses*, is pervaded by amorous encounters, scenes in bordellos, feasts of lanterns, astrological lore, spells and aphrodisiac material, bawdry and cuckoldry, erotic techniques and sexual stimuli including the Monk's Pill, ointments, instruments, silver clasp and sulphur ring, a white silk ribbon with medicinal properties to increase desire, as well as constant references to the power of perfumes. Among the large number of characters are Golden Lotus herself, Porphyry, and Hsi-mên Ch'ing, young boys and old knowledgeable beldames familiar with every lubricity, every love charm and potion.

Chocolate

In eighteenth century France, many aphrodisiac dishes and pastries were compounded with chocolate.

Cocoa, on the other hand, has been held to be anti-aphrodisiac.

Yet the belief in the aphrodisiac value of chocolate prevailed for a long time. In the seventeenth century, monks in France were forbidden to drink chocolate on account of its reputed amatory properties.

Chorier

Nicolas Chorier (1612-1692). Author of Satyre Sodatique sur les Arcanes de l'amour et de Vénus en sept dialogues,

L'Escarmouche

Tribadison
Anatomie
Le Duel
Voluptés
Amours
Fescennins
Edited by Bagneux de Villeneuve in the Bibliothèque
des Curieux, Paris, 1910.

Chrysocolla
Etymologically, this expression, derived from Greek,
means gold glue.

It is a nostrum recommended for aphrodisiac purposes in
The Perfumed Garden.

Eat chrysocolla, advised the author, the Sheik Nefzawi.
It is the size of a mustard-grain.

Chrysocolla is a substance that was used in soldering
metals. It has been suggested that in all probability it is
borax.

See *PERFUMED GARDEN.*

Chutney
A relish compounded of herbs, fruits, and various season-
ings. Commonly in use in the Orient, it has a reputation for
stimulating the libido.

Cider
Credited with aphrodisiac virtue.

Often mentioned, fictionally, in scenes involving amatory
encounters.

Cinchona
A Peruvian bark that is used as a tonic. It has frequently
been credited with the property of stimulating erotic expression.

Cincia
Also called Cinxia. A Roman goddess to whom the girdle
of the bride was consecrated, symbolic of sexual surrender.

Cinnamon

The dried inner bark of an East India tree. Used as a spice with reputed erotic effects.

Your products are a park of pomegranates . . . Nard and saffron, calamus and cinnamon.

Song of Songs 4.14

Cinnamon Liqueur

Centuries ago, this drink was famous as an aphrodisiac but has gone out of use.

Circus Maximus

This arena, the scene of public racing contests, was, among the Romans, a kind of hotbed of incitements, by the very nature of the sadistic characteristics of these performances, to sexual expression. Hence, as a vast and turbulent outlet, the proximity of numberless prostitutes who were lodged in this area of the city.

The Church Fathers, particularly Tertullian and Augustine, inveigh against these practices, in which both betting on the results of the chariot races and wild promiscuities were involved.

Luxorius, a poet of the fifth century A.D., has left a large number of poems descriptive of these activities. Like these activities themselves, the poems are obscene and perverted.

Civet

A perfume derived from the civet-cat. The French royal court used to offer sweets, perfumed with civet, to desirable ladies.

Civet-cats were bred for their secretions that formed the base of perfumes and were also of aphrodisiac value.

It is of interest to note that Daniel Defoe, author of *Robinson Crusoe,* was for a time the owner of a civet-cat farm.

Clams

Reputed to possess marked aphrodisiac virtue.

Most kinds of sea-food have been credited with this property.

Clauder, Gabriel

Author of a dissertation, *De Philtris*, published in 1661.

Clauder discusses, historically and medically, the uses of philtres and potions of various kinds. Some were concocted for poisoning purposes, others, for amatory effects. Among the ingredients mentioned by Clauder are laurel and olive leaves, milk, saliva.

Clearchus

Clearchus of Soli, in Cyprus, an ancient Greek writer of the third century B.C. Author of an amatory treatise entitled *Erotica,* an analysis of the nature of love, accompanied by numerous historical and mythological instances. Some of this material is still extant in the citations of other writers.

Cleopatra

Precious stones were always associated with magic properties, sometimes apotropaic, to ward off various evils and misfortunes that constantly beset mankind, and, on occasion, aphrodisiac in intent. Thus pearls were traditionally endowed with aphrodisiac virtues. There was a legend that Cleopatra was accustomed to dissolve pearls in vinegar and drink the fluid in order to provoke her amorousness.

See *AGATE*.

Clothing

In ancient Sparta girls wore a tunic ending above the knees and slit high at the side, for this reason these girls were known as thigh-showers. This was a visual means of erotic enticement.

The Roman satirist Varro describes a huntress whose dress was tucked up so high as to display a posterior exposed view, *non modo suris apertis, sed paene natibus apertis ambulans.*

Cocaine

This is a dangerous habit-forming drug, whose use provokes sexual desire and amatory excitement in both sexes, but particularly in women. Habituation leads to all manner of sexual perversions and a break down in all moral restraints. Without medical advice it should never be used.

Cockles

Considered to have stimulating aphrodisiac properties.

Many kinds of sea-food have traditionally been so considered. The Greek encyclopedist, Athenaeus, author of *The Banquet of the Philosophers,* mentions the efficacy of sea-foods in this respect.

Cod Liver

Reputed to be a marked amatory stimulant.

Most fish, in fact, are reputed to have this virtue.

Cod Roe

Considered a sexual stimulant.

Coffee as an Anti-Aphrodisiac

Coffee is said to dull the sexual urge. A seventeenth century traveler in Persia describes the Khan as smoking a narghileh. In addition, the Khan drinks a kind of black liquid called Kahowa (that is, coffee) that seems to be a deterrent to lasciviousness.

Coitus

Speaking of the customs prevalent in India in connection with erotic practices, Nefzawi, the author of *The Perfumed Garden,* enumerates twenty-nine modes of intimacy.

See *PERFUMED GARDEN.*

Cola

An extensively used refreshing drink. It is also known as bichy. It is obtained from the dried seeds of a plant called *Cola Nitida*. The seeds or nuts are common in Africa, where they are used as currency and often as charms and sacred objects.

Cola is chewed by the natives, and is believed to endow them with vigor. It is also reputedly a sexual stimulant.

Colewort

Among the Romans, this herb was associated with lascivious activities and was dedicated to the phallic god Priapus.

Collyrium

A Latin term meaning *eye-salve*. Such salves, in use both among the Romans and the Hindus, were conceived to have stimulating value in sexual relationships.

In addition, collyrium was endowed traditionally with magic properties conducive to amatory expression.

Comment on Love

Plautus, the Roman comedy writer, in one of his plays, *Trinummus*, cautions the lover. Love, he is told, is soft-spoken yet greedy, corruptive, ruthless, and lying.

See *PLAUTUS*.

Commerce in Aphrodisiacs

Lizards, reputed to be of high aphrodisiac potency, used to be brought by Egyptian fellahin to Cairo, then shipped to the Mediterranean ports, particularly Marseilles and Venice, where they were much sought after.

Concubine

Among the Romans, sexual diversions, in the form of concubinage, were not frowned upon socially or publicly. Even on epitaphs women are described, without contempt, as having been concubines.

Condemnation of Love

Valerius Maximus, a Roman historian of the first century A.D., inveighs violently against love,

What is more shameful than lust?

What is more destructive?

Similarly, Philo Iudaeus, who belongs in the first century A.D., says,

There is nothing so contradictory as love and knowledge.

Cordax

An indecent Greek dance, provoking sensual desires.

There was a Greek divinity named Artemis Cordaka, in whose honor such a dance was performed in Elis.

The dance consisted of sexual exhibitionism, reeling and swaying as if in a state of intoxication, erotic bodily movements, and denudation.

Coriander

Albertus Magnus, the thirteenth century philosopher and occultist, states that coriander, valerian, and violet are love producing herbs. They must, however, be gathered in the last quarter of the moon.

Corinth

In ancient times, this Greek port was notorious for its vast, ingenious, and expensive licentiousness. Horace, the Roman poet, makes this admission,

It is not everyone who can (afford to) go to Corinth.

In addition to the swarms of prostitutes and hetairae, there were numberless brothels and a temple dedicated to Aphrodite, attended by a thousand hierodouloi.

See *HIERODOULOI*.

Corpse

A Hindu prescription. Flowers thrown on a human corpse that is being carried out to a burning ghat, together with a mixture of the leaf of the Indian plant vatodbhranta,

68

and the powdered bones of the jiwanjiva bird and the peacock. This compound, when applied to the lingam, results
in sexual dominance.

Countercharms

When anaphrodisiac enchantments were effected on a
victim, there was some redress at hand. Countercharms could
be used. One such prescribes a virgin parchment, on which,
before sunrise, and for nine successive days, the word
ARIGAZARTOR was to be inscribed.

Another charm recommended,

Pronounce the word TEMON three times at sunrise,
on a day that gives promise of heralding fine weather.

Courtesans

The courtesan in ancient times was such a normal social
feature of life that among the Greeks and the Romans there
are at least fifty terms to describe a courtesan, according to
social status, location, appearance, and so on. In connection
with this situation, there were state taxes, tax collectors, and
city supervision.

Lucian, the Greek satirist of the second century A.D.,
wrote witty pieces entitled *Dialogues of Courtesans*.

The *Letters of Courtesans*, by Alciphron, who also belongs to the second century A.D., indicate how familiar and
widespread and accepted the fact of prostitution was in Greek
times.

Cow Wheat

Melampryum Pratense. A tall plant, with yellowish
flowers. Used as food for cows. But Pliny the Elder, the
Roman encyclopedist, and Dioscorides the physician say
that it inflames the amatory passions.

Crab Apples

Often made into jellies and preserves and so reputed to
have a stimulating effect.

Crabs

The Greeks considered them as aphrodisiacs.
See *SHELL-FISH*.

Crayfish

Particularly in the Mediterranean littoral crayfish are considered of high aphrodisiac potency. Boiled in oil, with pepper, salt, garlic, and other spices, crayfish will reputedly provoke amatory urges.

Cress

A solitary plant, growing among ruins, old walls, in the fields. Used for salads, and as an aphrodisiac eaten raw, or boiled, or drunk as a juice. The plant is cultivated in the East for its sexual value.

Ovid, Martial, and Columella, all Roman poets, testify to its erotic power. Hence it was called *impudica, shameless.* Marcellus Empiricus, a Roman physician, prescribed three scruples of cress, three of red onion, three of pine seed, three of Indian nard, for impotence.

Apicius, author of a Roman cookbook, recommends, for the consummation of desire, onions cooked in water, with pine seeds or cress juice and pepper.

Crete

On the island of Crete, in ancient times, a festival was held in honor of the god Hermes, at which all kinds of sexual indulgence were granted. The entire spectacle thus constituted a kind of general aphrodisiac stimulant.

Crocodile

Crocodile teeth, asserts Pliny the Elder, in his vast storehouse of ancient knowledge, the *Historia Naturalis,* attached to the right arm, will act as an aphrodisiac.

It must be remembered that such an item was rarely, if at all, tested by the compiler. Hence the accumulation, in the course of centuries, of numberless untried, traditional recipes.

70

Crocodile Tail
The tail of young crocodile is a sexual delicacy.

The Roman poet Horace states that the excrement of the crocodile has aphrodisiac virtues.

Cteis
A Hindu synonym for the yoni, the pudenda muliebria.

Cubeb
The cubeb, indigenous to Java, is a berry similar to a grain of pepper, with a pungent flavor. Used in cookery and medicine.

A drink made from cubeb pepper is described as a strong aphrodisiac known to the Arabs.

Chewing cubeb pepper also produces similar results, so with powdered cubeb mixed with honey.

In China, an infusion of cubeb pepper leaves is prepared as a highly stimulating aphrodisiac.

The eating of cubebs as a sexual inducement is suggested by the thirteenth century Arab philosopher and physician Avicenna.

Ctesippus
A Greek who was reputed to be so voluptuous that he was said to have sold the stones from his father's grave in order to indulge his lusts.

Cucumber
Probably on account of its phallic formation, the cucumber is often assumed to have aphrodisiac qualities.

Cumin
An aromatic plant used as a condiment and credited with erotic stimulus.

Cuminum Cyminum
Cumin. An aromatic plant similar to fennel. Has, reputedly, aphrodisiac qualities.

71

Cure

According to Arab erotology, a cure for amatory inadequacy consists of physical health, absence of worry, equanimity, wholesome food, mental tranquillity, wealth, and a variety of female faces and complexions.

Curry

An oriental dish flavored with spices. Reputedly a sexual stimulant.

Cuttle-Fish

Cuttle-fish, spiced oysters, sea hedge-hogs, and lobsters were among the ingredients of love-potions that the reputed thaumaturgist Apuleius, who lived in the second century A.D., was accused of having prepared in order to win the love of a widow.

There is a great deal of material on this subject in Apuleius' defense speech, *De Magia*, which is still extant.

Cyclamen

The root of the cyclamen, sowbread, was used in ancient times as an ingredient in love potions.

Damiana

This drug is obtained from the dried leaves of a plant called *turnera diffusia* or *turnera aphrodisiaca*.

The plant is a shrub that grows in the lowlands of Brazil, it is also found abundantly in Bolivia and Mexico and is also cultivated in California. Damiana is a powerful stimulant with aphrodisiac effects.

Dancing

The ancient Romans frowned upon dancing, especially by women, as they considered it an erotic inducement. One Roman historian, Sallust, comments that a certain Sempronia danced more gracefully than a respectable woman should.

The Roman poet Ovid, author of the *Ars Amatoria*, recommends dancing to all girls who are in love.

At banquets and public performances of various kinds professional dancing-girls appeared. Generally, they were imported from Spain or Syria. Skilled in erotic movements and manipulations, they readily provoked the sensual desires of the spectators. The Roman satirist Juvenal describes them as writhing and wriggling frantically to the musical accompaniment of their own castanets, to excite sluggish lovers. Other Roman poets, among them Propertius, Horace, and the epigrammatist Martial say similar things about the amatory provocations of such dancers.

Lascivious Ionic dances, too, although condemned by grave elders, were popular among Roman girls.

Dangers of Herbs

Only by prolonged tests of trial and error have the

beneficent or toxic properties of plants been determined.

An apposite illustration occurs in Biblical literature,

And the sons of the prophets were sitting before him, and he said unto his servant, Set on the great pot, and seethe pottage for the sons of the prophets.

And one went out into the fields to gather herbs, and found a wild vine, and gathered thereof wild gourds his lap full, and came and shred them into the pot of pottage, for they knew them not.

So they poured out for the men to eat. And it came to pass, as they were eating of the pottage, that they cried out, and said, O thou man of God, there is death in the pot. And they could not eat thereof.

II Kings 4.38, 39, 40.

Darnel

A grass that, if sprinkled with frankincense, myrrh, and barley meal, was reputed to be a sexual aid for women.

Dates

Preserved dates are by some gourmets believed to possess erotic stimulus.

Davenport

John Davenport, author of two series of essays dealing with curious anthropological and sexual conditions. Their titles are *Aphrodisiacs and Anti-Aphrodisiacs* and *Curiositates Eroticae Physiologiae*. Rare, privately printed volumes, published late in the nineteenth century.

Deer Sperm

In ancient times, this was used as an ingredient in aphrodisiac concoctions. An example of organotherapy.

See *ORGANOTHERAPY*.

De La Mare

William de la Mare, a French writer who published in

Paris, in 1512, *De Tribus Fugiendis Ventre, Pluma et Venere Libelli Tres.*

The book deals with excesses in food, sleep, and sex.

Demetrius

Demetrius of Phalerum, a peripatetic philosopher of the fourth century B.C., wrote an amatory treatise entitled *Eroticus*—no longer, however, extant.

Democritus

An ancient Greek philosopher who was credited with mixing love draughts.

Devices of Courtesans

Greek and Roman courtesans made aphrodisiacs with pepper, myrrh, two perfumes called Cyprian and Egyptian. The cups for drinking were made of scented earthenware.

Diasatyrion

According to Venette, diasatyrion root taken morning and night with a little wine or cow's milk, for an entire week, will rejuvenate even old men.

In the inns of Persia a viscous drink was sold, the base of which was satyrion. Called by the Persians syrup of fox.

See *VENETTE.*

Dictionnaire Erotique

A Latin-French erotic dictionary produced by Nicolas Blondeau and published by Liseux in Paris, in 1885.

Diet

The importance of a diet as a sexual factor is abundantly attested in the ancient writers. In his poem *De Rerum Natura* the Roman poet Lucretius says,

Another important consideration is the diet that sustains you, for some foods make the seeds grow thick in the limbs and other foods in turn thin them and weaken them.

75

In Chinese tradition, proper diet is conducive not only to bodily health but also to continued sexual activity. The Chinese too consider that excess, both in eating and drinking, emotional anxieties, grief are of anti-aphrodisiac intent.

Dill
Michael Drayton (1563-1631), the English poet, refers to the stimulating effect of dill in potions.

Diminution of Libido
A Hindu prescription recommended to achieve this condition is an application consisting of the juice of the fruits of the cassia fistula, eugenia jambolana, mixed with powder of soma plant, vernonia anthelmintica, the eclipta prostata, the lohopa-jihirka. These plants are of course indigenous to India.

Diodorus Siculus
A Greek historian of the first century B.C. who says, of the ancient witch Circe,

None knew better the various natures of plants and their marvelous properties.

Among these plants and herbs were such as to arouse amatory activity.

Dionysia
A Greek festival in honor of Dionysus, god of wine and fertility. At the rural festival, huge ithyphalli were carried around in solemn public procession, symbolic of the spirits of fruitfulness. The result among the spectators was a pronounced erotic stimulus.

Dionysius
Tyrant of Sicily. In the city of Locris he filled a house with wild thyme, an aphrodisiac, and roses, and, summoning the young women of the city he practised orgiastic obscenities with them.

Dionysus

Ancient god of wine and fertility. The phallus was dominant in the Dionysiac cult. In Lesbos the god was worshipped as Dionysus Phallen. In the island of Rhodes a phallic festival, the Phallophoria, was celebrated with erotic orgiastic accompaniments.

To Dionysus were dedicated the ass, the panther, the bull, and the goat.

Dissertation on Oysters

In 1821 appeared a French dissertation on the properties of the green oyster of Marennes.

See *OYSTERS*.

Dissoluteness

In one of his plays the Greek comedy writer Aristophanes frankly mentions, as a characteristic of a dissolute youth, a kolain megalain, *magnum membrum virile*.

Dog-Stones

A species of the plant satyrion (orchis mascula) that was formerly reputed to possess aphrodisiac properties.

Doubles Entendres

In modern burlesque, and in ancient Greek romantic tales, of which several are extant *in toto*, sexual and erotic stimuli are often present in concealed and ambivalent doubles entendres.

Dove

Dove's brains have been prepared by chefs for amorous expectations.

Dragon's Blood

A plant used as a love charm.

It was wrapped in paper and thrown on the fire, to the accompaniment of a rhyming couplet,

> May he no pleasure or profit see
> Till he comes back again to me.

Dramatists

The plays of the English Restoration dramatists abound in references to the popularity and use of erotic powders and aphrodisiac herbs.

Drepang: Also Tripang

A Malay term. It is a species of holothuria or sea slug. Found in the Red Sea and in Oceania. On manual contact, this cucumber shaped object expands, symbolical of genital tumescence. Among the Arabs it is a highly popular aphrodisiac. Also greatly prized by the Chinese, to whom it is imported after the drepang is dried in the sun.

Dried Frog

An early medical writer, Alexander Benedictus, asserts that a powder made from dried frog induced a disgust for amatory exercises.

Dried Liver

This was used by the Romans as an ingredient in love potions. Horace, the Roman poet, makes mention of this fact in one of his Epodes,

That his parch'd marrow might compose,
Together with his liver dried, an amorous dose.

Drinking

In all ages wine drinking, in addition, as the Greeks declared, to being a poetic inspiration, was a preliminary to sexual aggressiveness.

Theophrastus, a Greek philosopher of the 3rd century B.C., wrote a treatise on the virtues of *Drunkenness*.

Drugs

In the continuous and frantic search for invigorating and rejuvenating sexual processes, drugs have presented tempting, wishful possibilities. Many of these drugs, however, both in their natural form or synthetically prepared, are either dangerous to take without proper medical advice or are ineffective for the purpose intended but produce other indirect and harmful effects.

Du Barry

Among ingredients of aphrodisiac dishes associated with Madame du Barry are ginger omelettes, stuffed capon, terrapin soup, sweetbreads, shrimp soup, crawfish.

Dudaim

The Biblical term for mandrake. This root has been identified with various plants, roots, herbs. Some authorities equate it with raspberries, also with fruit of the Zizyphus, the Spina Christi of Linnaeus. Others attribute to it the properties of truffles.

Du Four De La Crespeliere

A seventeenth century French physician who wrote a series of poems and burlesque pieces entitled *Les Divertissements d'Amour*. Here he also discussed the amatory effects of wine and foods under the heading Le Triomphe du Roy-Boit, *The Triumph of King Drink*.

Dufz

A perfume used by Arabs as an aphrodisiac stimulant.

Dust to Dust

Among the Bretons of France, it was an old custom for the women, after religious services, to gather the dust in the chapel and blow it over a reluctant lover, in the confident expectation of the aphrodisiac effect of the action.

E

Echites

Also called *Aquileus,* because it is found in eagles' nests, purple in color, it contains another stone in it. Found near Ocean's shores and in Persia. Conducive to generate love. Albertus Magnus, *De Secretis Mulierum.*

Eels

Like most marine life, eels are said to possess aphrodisiac properties. In this regard eel soup is a highly favored dish.

Efficacy of Borax

In regard to the effect of borax, Dr. Venette adds,

Il pénètre toutes les parties de notre corps et en ouvre tous les vaisseaux, et par la ténuité de sa substance, il conduit aux parties genitales tout ce qui est capable de nous servir de matière à la semence.

See *VENETTE.*

Efficacy of Mint

According to the erotologist Mattioli, this herb is effective in strengthening male vigor.

Effluvia

The power of certain aromas and odors to excite venereal desires is evident not only in human beings, but in nearly all the mammals as well, and also among the "inferior animals."

Most mammifera exhale, in the rutting season, peculiar emanations serving to announce to the male the presence of the female, and to excite in him the sexual desire. This situation is true also in the case of insects, for example, in the female of the bombyx butterfly, which, although enclosed in a hermetically sealed box, will excite and invite the approach of the males.

Egg
The yolk of an egg in a small glass of cognac, drunk every morning, has been popular as an aphrodisiac in France. In Morocco, love philtres are composed of yolk of egg and bedbugs.

Oriental dishes intended as aphrodisiacs frequently contain eggs as an ingredient.

Egg yolks are recommended by an Arab erotologist as an energetic sexual stimulant.

Another potent Arab dish is a mass of eggs fried in fat and butter, then cooked and soaked in honey. This is eaten with a small piece of bread.

The Perfumed Garden says that he who eats the yolk of three eggs every day will be sexually invigorated. A similar stimulant is eggs boiled with pepper, cinnamon, and myrrh.

See *PERFUMED GARDEN*.

Egg Drink
A highly potent drink consists of eggs, milk, salt, brandy, sugar or honey. Compounded into an egg flip.

Egyptian Enticements
To induce amatory urges, the ancient Egyptians pursued an elaborate and regular ritual. Three baths a day were a household routine, to ensure total cleanliness. The dress of the women was diaphanous, the body being veiled subtly to arouse the erotic impulse.

Depilatories were used for all hirsute parts of the body. The body was perfumed, and then treated with cosmetics. For the eyes, to enhance their glow, plant juices were applied. Finally, ornaments— gold, jewels, armlets—were added to increase the visual attraction and the sensual inclinations.

Eighteenth Century

This century was particularly marked, throughout Europe, especially in France, and also in England, as an age of licentiousness, both in social life, at court and among the peasantry, in poetry and on the stage. Hence the extended search for aphrodisiac means and the interest in gastronomic matters, which it became increasingly evident, produced impacts on the *vita sexualis*.

Emblem of Generation

Long before the Christian era the cross, in a variety of forms, was associated with mystic, religious, erotic rites.

In some countries, particularly in Egypt, the cross has been considered, and so represented, as a reproductive symbol. So also in Tibet and in central Asian territory.

The Egyptian crux ansata, common on Egyptian monuments and other memorials, is considered by some authorities as a triple phallus.

It is thought that there is a reference to the crux ansata in the Bible,

And the Lord said unto him, Go through the midst of the city, through the midst of Jerusalem, and set a mark upon the foreheads of the men that sigh and that cry for all the abominations that be done in the midst thereof.

Ezekiel 9.4.

Emblica

Avicenna, thirteenth century Arab philosopher and physician, recommends honey of emblica as an aphrodisiac. It may here be noted that not all of the roots, plants, herbs mentioned in ancient or Oriental literature have been botanically identified.

Emblica Myrabolans

According to the *Kama Sutra,* an ointment composed of this plant, will have aphrodisiac value.

82

Enchanted Aphrodisiac

The *Kama Sutra,* the Hindu erotic manual, recommends the following recipe,

A bead, made of the seed of jujube or of conch shell, enchanted by magic incantation, then tied to the hand.

Endive

Used as love charm by girls in Germany.

Endive, like a number of similar plants, is both esculent and reputed to have some aphrodisiac property.

Enticement

Thomas Dekker (c. 1572—c. 1632), in his comedy *The Shoemaker's Holiday,* refers to magic practices for the purpose of winning love,

Jane,

Good sir, I do believe you love me well;
For 'tis a silly conquest, silly pride
For one like you—I mean a gentleman—
To boast that by his love-tricks he hath brought
Such and such women to his amorous lure;
I think you do not so, yet many do,
And make it even a very trade to woo.
I could be coy, as many women be, ·
Feed you with sunshine smiles and wanton looks,
But I detest witchcraft.

Eonism

One of the most notorious transvestists was a certain Chevalier d'Eon. During the eighty three years of his life, he presented a puzzle to both French and English society. For years at a time he lived, alternately, as a man and as a woman. On his death his male sex was discovered.

The term Eonism has been applied to this perversion. It is a synonym of transvestism.

See *TRANSVESTISM.*

Eos

Eos, goddess of dawn, was, in Greek mythological tradition, an intensely amorous divinity. Whoever came within her favorable and passionate notice was grasped and carried off amorously. Among them were the youths Tithonus, Ceppalus, Orion, and Cleitus.

Such a myth, like many others popular among the Greeks, had its sensual provocative effect on the erotic inclinations of the Greeks themselves.

Eros

Eros, the god of love, was pandemic among the Greeks. In the Greek gymnasium, where the young men exercised naked, and where poets, philosophers and others met in the surrounding halls, baths, and colonnades, there was a prominent statue of Eros, as well as other sculptural pieces representing the divinities.

Erotic Climax

In chapter five of *The Perfumed Garden* Nefzawi describes the attitudes and emotions of both men and women in actu sexuali.

See *PERFUMED GARDEN.*

Erotic Cookery

In the Convent of Sainte-Marie-des Bois, a fictional retreat of libidinous monks described by the Marquis de Sade in his novel *Justine,* the author refers to the practice of flagellation and voyeurism on the part of these monks. Plentiful meals are also his theme, pies and turkey garnished with truffles, games and pastries, fruits, creams, preserves, wines, liqueurs—accompanied by excess in both eating and drinking and all designed to encourage sexual excitations resulting in indiscriminate orgies after the meals.

See *FLAGELLATION, VOYEURISM.*

From *Johannes Scherr Germania,* Stuttgart: Speman, 1883-84

PLATE 5—Johannes Faustus
(Etching by Rembrandt)

D. MIGUEL MAÑARA
VICENTELO DE LECA.

PLATE 6—Don Miguel Mañara Vicentelo de Leca
(from an old illustration)
This portrait is believed to be that of the historical, not the legendary, Don Juan.

Erotic Dances

The Greek historian Herodotus describes an incident involving a sexual, arousing dance. The ruler of Sicyon, Cleisthenes, had a beautiful daughter named Agariste. Numerous suitors appeared in turn, all unsuccessfully. Then appeared Hippoclides, a wealthy young Athenian. He arrived at a banquet arranged by Cleisthenes himself. Having drunk heavily, Hippoclides mounted the table and performed a number of lewd dances. Cleisthenes, shocked, exclaimed, "You have danced away your bride."

The names of such lascivious, sexually provoking performances are known to us. One was the Dance of the Callabides, another, the Sicinnis, that involved stripping off the clothes as well as obscene movements.

Erotic Effect of Dancing

Ovid, the amatory poet, describes a professional dancing-girl, whose subtle bodily movements are such an excitant as to provoke, in an ascetic such as the ancient Hippolytus, a priapean condition.

See *PRIAPUS*.

Erotic Effects of Diet

Many types of food, by empirical practice, have been traditionally associated with erotic virtues. Of all such foods, fish, rich in phosphorus, have since antiquity onward maintained a primary role in accredited amatory diet.

Eroticism in Sanskrit

Sanskrit poetry and drama contain practical and specific descriptions, counsel, prescriptions, and general guidance in sexual matters in the widest sense.

Men and women are methodically divided into classes, according to occupation, age, conduct, temperament. So with women. These categories are commented on with scrupulous precision so that sexological matters assume a totally scientific form, free from haphazard conjectures and dubieties.

Erotic Festival

In ancient Greece, the five-day festival of the Thesmophoria was celebrated, by women only, in honor of the two goddesses Persephone and Demeter. This was symbolically a propagation rite and involved women, married life, and propagation. In the course of time the festival spread through all the colonies of Greece, to Sicily, the shores of the Black Sea, and Asia Minor.

In Attica, the women participants were required to observe sexual abstinence for nine days before the festival. The ostensible reason, said the priests, was an act of piety, but actually the abstinence merely goaded toward unrestrained sexual orgies.

Erotic Provocations

The Arab erotologist, the Sheik Nefzawi, says,

The kiss on the mouth, on the two cheeks, upon the neck, as well as the sucking up of fresh lips, are gifts of God.

These amatory expressions, he adds, provoke further activity.

See *PERFUMED GARDEN*.

Erotic Religious Mysteries

At Paphos in Cyprus, a Greek festival was held annually in honor of Aphrodite, goddess of love. Men and women participated in the ceremonies, which were characterized by orgiastic sexual rites. The Roman Fathers of the Church, among them Clement of Alexandria and Arnobius, centuries later, fulminated against these pagan rites.

The initiated member gave a gift of a coin for the goddess, for which he received in turn a phallus and some salt.

Erotic Sale

In the ancient city of Isernia, in the Kingdom of Naples, as late as the eighteenth century an annual three-day fair was held. At this festival wax reproductions of the male genitalia were publicly exposed for sale. These images were usually purchased by barren women as a hopeful means of erotic stimulus.

Erotic Songs

Such songs, both popular and scholarly, were common in all countries, in every age. Bawdy, forthright, suggestive, they were all indirect stimulants. One such old French chant runs as follows,

> Brûlez-le des plus vives flammes,
> S'il faut contenter six cents femmes,
> Quelque soit le tempérament,
> Ça doit gêner sur le moment.

Erotic Symbols

To Aphrodite, goddess of love in ancient mythology, the ram, the hare, the dove, the sparrow and the goat were all sacred. Their significance lay in the fact that they all had particularly amorous natures, so that in a more generalized sense, whatever promoted the concept of prolific sexual expression was welcome and dedicated to the goddess.

The prevalence of this notion was so widespread that the coins of Cyprus presented the image of the ram.

In Athens, the goddess was known as Aphrodite Epitragia (that is, Aphrodite on a Goat).

In the goddess' temples doves were kept and cared for by the attendants.

In the Roman novelist Apuleius' *Metamorphoses* Aphrodite rides in a car drawn by four doves, with an accompaniment of sparrows and other birds.

In a poem by Sappho, Aphrodite is represented as riding in a car drawn by sparrows.

Erotic Stimulants

An ancient writer lists the means by which women, young and old, entice the sexual ardor of men. Their amatory reinforcements consist of boxes of powder for whitening the teeth and blackening the eyebrows, hair dyes, hair curlers, colored sandals, diaphanous robes, heavy earrings and armlets, gold necklaces, rouge, grease-paint.

Erotic Tales

Every age has its literary erotic stimulants, to whet the popular appetite or to imprint in permanence the basic ethnic legends that centre around the primary and universal procreative principle. Sometimes these sagas and anecdotes are touched with ribaldry, or with excessive obscenity, according to the times, and sometimes they are rooted in obscure but still verifiable deistic concepts.

Among the Greeks, the amatory tales of Pherecydes of Syros, of which, however, only fragments are extant, the digressive anecdotes in Herodotus' *History of the Persian Wars*, the amatory collection entitled *Milesian Tales*, produced by Aristides of the first century B.C., the love romance narrated by Ctesias the physician, are among the significant contributions to the erotic genre. Among the Romans, the famous picaresque novel of the *Satyricon*, by Petronius, as well as the adventurous and libidinous *Metamorphoses of* Apuleius, are particularly notable. Later ages contributed in their own epichorial and distinctive manner to these universal delights in the erotic. In China, *The Golden Lotus* is an amazing sustained achievement.

Boccaccio's *Decameron* in Italy, *The Arabian Nights* in the Moslem world, Walter Map's *De Nugis Curialium,* especially the tale of the two merchants, and the Turkish folk tales with their wild buffoon-like but shrewd protagonist have become incorporated in the stream of world literature. France added a not inconsiderable quota. Restif de la Bretonne produced *Les Contemporains,* early in the nineteenth century.

88

Paul de Kock, who died in 1871, followed with a large number of erotic tales, of which *La Pucelle de Belleville* was a characteristic example. The *Contes Drôlatiques* of Honoré de Balzac and the *Contes Cruels* of Villiers de L'Isle-Adam all testify to man's continuous interest and absorption in erotic matters.

Erotic Views

The Greeks cultivated an intense enjoyment of life, particularly the amatory delights. The Greek philosopher Empedocles is said to have declared that once mankind knew only one divinity, the goddess of love.

Even the divinities resorted to aphrodisiac devices as sexual stimulants. In Homer's *Iliad,* the goddess Hera uses amatory stimuli to charm Zeus, her husband. Hera begs the goddess of love, Aphrodite, for 'the magic girdle of love and longing, which subdues the hearts of all the gods and of mortal dwellers upon earth.'

Aphrodite accedes to the request, "and loosed from her bosom a broidered girdle, wherein are fashioned all manner of allurements; therein is love, therein is longing and dalliance—beguilement that steals the wits of the wise."

(Loeb Classical Library)

Erotic Witchery

Bodin, the medieval demonographer, enumerates various methods of producing anaphrodisiac effects by enchantments.

The object was to render a prospective victim, an enemy, a husband or lover incapable of performing the conjugal rite. Cabalistic words—among them RIBALD and VANARBI—were to be pronounced. Mysterious diagrams and figures were traced with the left foot.

Wierus, De Lancre, Sprenger and other noted demonographers describe the procedures in great detail. The concept of prohibiting by occult means erotic intimacies was well known in ancient times. According to the Greek historian Herodotus, a certain Amasis was prevented from consummating amatory union with his wife Ladice through occult machinations.

Plato, the Greek philosopher, utters a warning to married persons in this regard. The Roman epic poet Vergil refers to the incapacitating effects of ligatures, while Ovid, the erotic poet, admits the power of such spell-bindings.

It was said of the Emperor Nero that, in a particular case when he displayed amatory incompetence, he exclaimed that he had been bewitched.

A certain Numantina, first wife of Plautius Sylvanus, was accused of having rendered her husband impotent by means of sorcery.

The corpus of ancient Roman law, The Twelve Tables, contained a prohibition against this practice.

The medieval historian, Gregory of Tours, mentions a spell put on a certain woman, who became the wife of Eulatius, by his concubines, who were driven by a spirit of jealousy. According to Paulus Aemilius, the medieval King Theodoric was incapacitated by witchcraft.

The practice was carried on, in a ribald spirit, in the European courts of Spain and Italy, during the Middle Ages.

The idling courtiers derived great amusement from these amatory frustrations and complications.

Er Roud El Aater P'nezaha El Khater

The Arabic title of *The Perfumed Garden* for the *Soul's Recreation*.

See *PERFUMED GARDEN*.

Eryngo

Eryngium maritimum, a herb known also as Sea Holly, Sea Hulver, and Sea Holme. It has the appearance of a thistle, with blue flowers. Its virtue lies in the fleshy root. For centuries, it was used as a powerful aphrodisiac. As a condiment, it now serves a similar purpose.

In Shakespeare's *The Merry Wives of Windsor* Falstaff mentions the root,

Hail kissing-comfits, and snow eringoes.

The root was candied and was reputed to stimulate potency and strengthen the genitalia.

In this form the Arabs knew it as an invigorating sexual stimulant for man and woman.

Dioscorides, an army physician who flourished in the first century A.D., treats it as an aid to digestion.

John Dryden, in his translation of the Roman satirist Juvenal, writes of the libertines

Who lewdly dancing at a midnight ball
For hot eryngoes and fat oysters call.

Euphorbium

A gum resin derived from a plant that is indigenous to North and to South Africa. According to Sinibaldus, it is mentioned by Avicenna as an aphrodisiac aid.

See *GENEANTHROPOEIA*.

Eusebius

A fourth century A.D. Greek writer who mentions a case of madness as the result of an aphrodisiac, but does not specify the identity of the stimulant.

In many cases, however, the ingredients of potions and unguents and similar compounds are described by the Greeks and Romans in adequate detail.

Excess

In reference to loss of virility and sexual excesses, Nefzawi, the author of the Arab *The Perfumed Garden,* asserts,

All sages and physicians agree in saying that the ills which afflict man originate with the abuse of coition. The man therefore who wishes to preserve his health, and particularly his sight, and who wants to lead a pleasant life, will indulge with moderation in love's pleasures, aware that the greatest evils may spring therefrom.

See *PERFUMED GARDEN*.

Excess of Aphrodisiacs

Sickness and even death not infrequently resulted from excessive doses of philtres and other aphrodisiac treatments. A courtesan once prepared a lavish dinner for a passionate young man. Every dish was spiced with cantharides. The guest, partaking eagerly of the feast, died the next day.

Exhalations

From various sources, both ancient and modern, bodily exhalations and contrived perfumes produce marked impacts on the erotic inclinations.

An early authority asserts,

Odors act powerfully upon the nervous system, they prepare it for all the pleasurable sensations, they communicate to it that slight disturbance or commotion which appears as if inseparable from emotions of delight, all which may be accounted for by their exercising a special action upon those organs whence originated the most rapturous pleasure of which our nature is susceptible.

Exhibitionism

A perversion that impels the exposure of the body, particularly the *membrum virile,* for sexual excitation.

External Applications

Liniments and other applications have been used externally to stimulate the libido. These washes and preparations were made of honey, liquid storax, oil, fresh butter, or the fat of the wild goose, together with a small quantity of spurge, pyrethrum, ginger, or pepper, with the further addition of a few grains of ambergris, musk, or cinnamon.

Eye

The Greeks, especially the dramatists Aeschylus, Sophocles, and Euripides, considered the eye as the gateway to love. Hence the marked effects of visual aphrodisiac representations on the beholder.

The poets describe the eye thus,

    The arrow of love sends the beams from the eyes.

Or,

    Eros drips desire from the eyes.

Or,

    the bewitching charm of the eyes.

F

Fakir

In India, fakirs used to be rendered impotent by a rigid regimen from childhood on. At the age of six or seven they were made to eat, daily, a quantity of young leaves called mairkousi. This treatment was continued until the age of twenty-five.

Falopia

An Italian writer, author of *Secreti Diversi et Miracolosi,* published in Venice in 1640. A section of the book deals with unguents, the preparation of ointments, electuaries, pills, and alchemical secrets.

Falstaff

Shakespeare's Falstaff calls philtres "medicines to make me love him."

Fascinum

A Latin term that is synonymous with phallus. Among the ancient Roman peasants, at harvest time or at the vintage, to celebrate the occasion—which was of course associated with fertility and productivity—there were festivities that took the form of chants motivated by the phallic theme, symbolical of cosmic creativeness.

Fatalities from Cantharides

Many instances are on record of the fatal results of the administration of this drug. Among the victims was Ferdinand of Castile, who died as a result of such a philtre.

Female Allure

Sometimes the cosmetics and similar preparations concocted by the ancients as erotic stimulants and beautifying aids failed of their purpose. This situation is well illustrated in a fragment of an old Greek comedy,

If you go out during the summer, two streams of dark paint flow from your eyes, and from your cheeks the sweat makes a red furrow down to your neck, and the hair on your forehead is grey, full of red lead.

Fennel

A fragrant plant used in sauces and believed to inspire sexual provocations.

A Hindu prescription for sexual vigor and at the same time a preservative of health contains these ingredients,

Juice of the fennel plant and milk mixed with honey, ghee, liquorice, and sugar. This compound is described as holy, partaking the essence of nectar.

Fennel soup is a dish used in some Mediterranean regions, reputed to stimulate desire.

Figs

Believed to possess aphrodisiac qualities.

Figs were anciently associated with phallic symbolism. Plutarch, the Greek biographer and philosopher, has this to say,

The festival of the Dionysia was anciently celebrated in a popular and lively manner. A wine-jar was carried round and also a vine-branch. Then someone brought forward a goat, and another a basket filled with figs; and over all, the phallus.

The fig was also symbolic of the lingam and the yoni. The French expression *faire la figue* means to make the obscene sexual gesture with two fingers and thumb. This gesture was well-known in the antique *lupanaria* of the Romans.

In a recent English novel the fig is made the thematic motif in a sexual drama.

95

Fish

Traditionally considered a powerful and unfailing erotic aid, particularly on account of the presence of phosphates and iodine. In the ancient Middle East certain cults had piscine deities, or deities with fish attributes of various kinds. The Roman poets chanted the praises of river and sea fish. Ausonius, for instance, has a poem on the Moselle River, about 150 verses being devoted to barbel, trout, turbot, and other fish associated with that river.

Catherine II of Russia, childless with her husband, the grandson of Peter the Great, was told by her Chancellor that the Empire urgently required an heir.

Imperialistic and realistic, Catherine ordered some caviar, and commanded her chef to prepare a fine sturgeon and Saltikoff, an officer of the guard, to be invited to dinner. The outcome of her forthright gastronomic decision was a healthy, acceptable heir.

Another historical anecdote, whether apocryphal or not, Saladin, to test the continence of some dervishes, invited two of them to his palace, and entertained them with rich food. They grew fat, but successfully resisted the enticing odalisques with whom they were confronted.

Surprised, Saladin changed the menu, serving only fish, excellently prepared, to the dervishes. Introduced once again to the odalisques, this time they succumbed.

Of particular interest as stimuli are carp and lobster, caviar and all kinds of roe, eel, salmon, mullet, tunny, herring, mackerel, plaice, whiting, and halibut.

According to Apuleius, fish were used in his days, and in other ages as love charms.

See *APULEIUS*.

In Egypt the aphrodisiac virtues of fish were so generally recognized that priests were forbidden to eat fish.

Fish and Venus

In antiquity, fish were credited with special aphrodisiac

virtues and efficacy in exciting women. A suggested explanation was that Venus herself was born of the sea. Her Greek name, Aphrodite, is associated with the Greek term *aphros*, which means foam.

Dr. Venette comments as follows, Nous avons l'expérience en France que ceux qui ne vivent presque que de coquillages et de poissons, qui ne sont que de l'eau rassemblée, sont plus ardents à l'amour que les autres. En effet, nous nous y sentons bien plus y portés en Caresme qu'en toute autre saison parce qu'en ce temps-là nous ne nous nourissons que de poissons et d'herbes qui sont des aliments composés de beaucoup d'eau.

See *VENETTE*.

Flagellation

Flagellation, especially among Orientals, is considered as much a sexual inducement as any other form of aphrodisiac. The procedure, of course, is not confined, and has never been confined, to the Orient.

Nicholas Venette, however, warns of the dangers of this practice.

See *VENETTE*.

In ancient Thessaly, the festival of Aphrodite Anosia, goddess of love, took place to the accompaniment of erotic flagellations.

In Sparta, boys were whipped at the altar of Artemis Orthia. Also, at the feast of Dionysus, in Arcadia, girls were exposed to a whipping, in both instances, sexual excitement was produced.

In modern times, the arch exponent of this type of sexual aberration was the so called Marquis de Sade. Frenzied scenes of fustigations appear in his *Histoire de Juliette*, published in six volumes in 1797.

See *MARQUIS DE SADE*.

Flea-Wort

The sap of this plant, according to Pliny the Elder,

author of *Historia Naturalis,* was an effective means of securing the birth of boys. Parents drank the sap three times daily, fasting for forty days.

The aphrodisiac significance of the plant is traditional.

Flowers

The aroma given off by flowers often has an aphrodisiac effect, especially on women. This is so particularly in the case of lilies of the valley, gardenia, frangipani, and henna.

Food

Proper, wholesome foods, particularly the normal dishes and recipes herein listed, are uniformly accepted as nutritious and energy-producing. Indirectly, wholesome food reacts favorably on the entire human organism and conduces to physiological and emotional balance.

Such a condition is consistently applauded as promotive of amatory interests.

Food of the Gods

Ancient Scandinavian legends describe apples as food of the gods. The belief was that the gods, grown old and decrepit, were rejuvenated by feasting on apples. There is possibly an allusion here to cider, as the acids in apples are also mentioned.

Forberg

Erotologist who produced a monumental *Manuel d' Erotologie Classique,* with Latin and French text. Published in Paris in 1887.

Fortuna Virilis

Man's Fortune. An ancient Roman goddess associated with sexual promiscuity, the cult of the phallus, and adultery.

Francis I

This sixteenth century king of France was known for his cultivated tastes, but also for his amatory adventures that were promoted by aphrodisiac drinks and foods. He was notorious for the number of his mistresses. He died exhausted by excesses.

Frangipane Cream
A pastry, consiting of Frangipane, spices and almonds, is recommended as a sexual aid in an Italian erotic cookery manual.

Frankincense
This is the perfume known also as olibanum. It is frequently mentioned in Biblical contexts, usually in association with erotic themes,

> sweet smelling frankincense . . .
> hill of frankincense . . .
> sweet odor of frankincense . . .

See *PERFUMES*.

French Aphrodisiacs
Among aphrodisiacs listed by Nicolas Venette are crayfish, cooked garlic, animal organs.
See *VENETTE*.

French Chronicler
An old French chronicler refers to a widespread custom of rendering a person incapable of amatory expression. The significant phrase was, nouer aiguillette, *to tie up the points,* i.e., to render the husband, by means of enchantments, incapable of the sexual rite. The French passage follows,

Quelques uns tiennent cela pour superstition, que quand on dit la Messe des espousées, lorsque l'on prononce ce mot Sara, à la bénédiction nuptiale, si vous estreignez une esguillette, que le marié ne pourra rien faire à son espousée la nuict suyvante, tant que la dite esguillette demeurera nouée.

Frequency of Indulgence
The Greek Zeno, founder of the Stoic philosophy, is

recorded to have had intimacy with his wife only once in his life, and that out of mere courtesy.

The philosophers Epicurus and Democritus were somewhat of the same opinion as Zeno.

The Greek athletes, to prevent their strength from being impaired, never married.

The Rabbis, anxious to preserve the racial integrity of their people, are said to have ordered, with a view to the prevention of loss of vigor, that a peasant should indulge once a week only, a merchant, once a month, a sailor, twice a year, and a scholar, once in two years.

The lawgiver Moses forbade indulgence before battle.

A French writer declared that,
les êtres qui font le plus abus de leurs facultés intellectuelles sont les moins capables d'un coït fréquent, tandis que les idiots, les crétins, l'exercent bien davantage.

Enfin les animaux à petit cerveau, tels que les poissons, montrent une extrême fécondité.

Frogs
Frogs, and the bones of frogs, were used among the Romans as aphrodisiacs.

Frogs' Legs
In many countries treated as a culinary delicacy, especially in France. Called by Norman Douglas a "noble aphrodisiac."

Fruit
Among fruits reputed to have stimulating qualities are, bananas, fresh figs, peaches, cherries, grapes.

Fumigation
In Hindu erotology, stress is laid on perfumed fumigation as a sexual stimulant.

Functional Activities
Functional scatological activities, involving defecation and urination, were, in Greek comedy and satire, sculpture,

vase painting and decoration closely linked with libidinous expression, licentious banquets, and erotic manifestations.

Functions of Aphrodisiacs

Aphrodisiacs have been used for a three-fold purpose, to restore the exhausted virility in men, or to arouse frigid women to sexual excitation, or to overcome cases of sterility.

G

Galanga

An Indian root used among Arabs as an aphrodisiac.

A compound of galanga, cubebs, sparrow wort, cardamoms, nutmeg, gillyflowers, Indian thistle, laurel seeds, cloves, Persian pepper is made into a drink. Taken twice daily morning and night, in pigeon or fowl broth, preceded and followed by water. The result, according to Arab tradition, is an effective aphrodisiac.

Gall

The gall of a jackal, among Arabs, was used as an aphrodisiac. It is specifically recommended as an ointment for this purpose by the Sheik Nefzawi, author of *The Perfumed Garden*.

Galopin

Dr. Auguste Galopin, author of *Le Parfum de la Femme et Le Sens Olfactif dans l'Amour*. Paris, 1889.

This is a study of the relation of perfumes to amatory inclinations.

See *PERFUMES*.

Game

Goose, duck, and pheasant are all credited with being stimulants in an erotic sense.

Garcias

A medieval writer who mentions a certain plant called *Bangue,* without any further reference or description, whose juice and leaves have aphrodisiac qualities.

Very probably *bangue* is a variant form of *bhang*.
See *BHANG*.

Garcilaso De La Vega

This traveler mentions that in the public squares of Mexico sexual bas-reliefs were common. Also, the reproductive act was worshipped under the symbols of the generative organs.

Similar bas-reliefs are found all over the territory of India, notably in the Caves of Ajanta.

Garlic

Of reputed aphrodisiac value, according to medical authority. Both European and Oriental erotologists include garlic as an aphrodisiac ingredient in foods.

Among the Ainu of Japan garlic was considered in the same category as the ancient Greek nectar and ambrosia of the gods.

Geneanthropoeia

A comprehensive textbook, in Latin, that is in the nature of a course in sexology and anatomy. The author is Johannes Benedict Sinibaldus, an Italian professor of medicine who published the book in Rome in 1642. Many chapters in the book deal with aphrodisiacs, especially from an historical viewpoint, and also contain numerous warnings against excessive amatory activity.

Genetyllides

In ancient Greek mythology, minor deities who presided over the act of generation. Dogs, being known for their lubricity, were regularly sacrificed to them.

Genital Adornments

Among some primitive tribal communities in East Indian islands and in South America, the men adorn the *membrum virile* with trinkets, rings, shells, and similar objects. The intention is to induce the most extreme orgiastic reactions in their mates.

Genitalia

In Biblical times, the genitalia were considered of such a sacred nature, as they are equally in Semitic countries, that oaths were made binding by reference to the member,

And Abraham said unto his eldest servant of his house, that ruled over all that he had, Put, I pray thee, thy hand under thy thigh,

And I will make thee swear by the Lord, the God of Heaven, and the God of the earth, that thou shalt not take a wife unto my son of the daughters of the Canaanites.

Genesis 24.2-3.

So also,

And the time drew nigh that Israel must die, and he called his son Joseph, and said unto him, If now I have found grace in thy sight, put, I pray thee, thy hand under thy thigh, and deal kindly and truly with me; bury me not, I pray thee, in Egypt.

Genesis 47. 29.

This type of oath is still in vogue in the Middle East.

Gentian Wine

Considered to have an aphrodisiac virtue and often, in a particularly erotic atmosphere, it has that property.

Ghee

In Hindu practice, ghee, which is clarified butter, is considered an aphrodisiac.

A Hindu manual of erotology suggests boiled ghee, drunk in the morning, in the spring time, as a healthful, strengthening beverage.

George IV

This English king so highly appreciated the genesiac virtues of truffles, that he gave his Foreign Ministers special directions. His Ministers at the Courts of Turin, Naples,

Florence, were emphatically counseled to forward to the Royal Kitchen any truffles that might be found superior in size, delicacy, or flavor.

Gillyflower

A clove-scented plant used as a condiment, a reputed aphrodisiac.

Ginger

Long known and used in the Far and Middle East in the native dietary.

In China, often used for medicinal purposes. A ginger-fruit jam is made among the Chinese and is credited with active sexual properties.

In Turkish, Indian, Arabian and other Oriental love recipes, ginger is frequently present as an ingredient in amatory concoctions, often, too, taken by mouth along with honey and pepper.

Ginseng

The root of *Panax ginseng*, grows in Korea and China, where it has long been known medicinally. The root resembles the male body, hence the association with potency in the restoration of virility.

Giton

A character in the *Satyricon*, the novel by the Roman Petronius. The name has become practically synonymous with a homosexual. Dr. Jacobus, describing the customs in China in the latter part of the nineteenth century, declares that in his time the practice was widespread, and implied no public shame. In Pekin, he adds, men are not ashamed to be seen in public with their Gitons, and in the theatres one may see the richest Chinese with their *amasii* standing behind their chair.

Dr. Jacobus states that the Tartars and the Mongolians are equally known for such practices.

The Arabs are particularly addicted to this vice. See, for instance, T. E. Lawrence's *Seven Pillars of Wisdom*.
See *JACOBUS*.

Goat

A Hindu prescription for achieving sexual activity,

A beverage prepared with the testicle of a goat or ram boiled in milk and sugar.

Anciently, the goat was associated with the goddess Aphrodite on account of its amorous tendencies, also to Dionysus, the god of fertility and procreation.

Pan, the sylvan deity who was attended by satyrs of highly sexual proclivities, was represented invariably with goat's feet, and was the special protector of goats.

Dioscorides, the first century, A.D. Greek physician who produced a valuable and long authoritative Materia Medica dealing with the properties of numberless plants and drugs, recommends, for excitation of the amatory impulse, fresh "boy-cabbage" steeped in goat's milk.

Goblets D'Amour

During the Renaissance, philtres, in France, called goblets d'amour, were obtainable from apothecaries, witches, and occultists. Ofen such goblets d'amour contained as ingredients the blood of a red-haired person, or the heart and tongue of vipers.

Goose

The goose was a symbol of potency. A passage in Petronius, author, of the *Satyricon,* describes the reaction as a result of killing a goose,

When the old woman saw the bird, she raised such a great shriek that you would have thought that the geese had come back into the room again. I was astonished and shocked to find so strange a crime at my door, and I asked her why she had flared up, and why she should be more sorry for the goose than for me. But she beat her hands together and said, "You villain, you dare to speak. Do you not know what a dreadful sin you have committed? You have killed the darling of Priapus, the goose beloved of all married women."

(Loeb Library)

Goose-Tongues

The Roman poet Ovid recommends goose-tongues for their aphrodisiac qualities.

This is also recommended in modern amatory cookery.

Gossypion

A tree whose juice, according to a medieval writer named Andreas Cisalpinus, was esteemed as an aphrodisiac.

Gourou

The native African term for the kola nut. This is really a large chestnut, like a horse chestnut. The natives of Senegal and the Sudan chew the gourou with delight, says an anthropologist, although it has a sharp and astringent taste. It produces a sort of general nervous excitement, which sensibly increases all the physical faculties, including of course the generative powers.

At the great *bamboulas* and fêtes the gourou is much used. It is a most valuable fruit when exceptionally hard work (amorous or otherwise) has to be done, but its use should not be abused.

Kola is now admitted into European therapeutics, and is used for restoring lost strength and stimulating the forces of the body. It contains a greater quantity of caffeine and theobromine than the best teas and coffees.

Graham

In the eighteenth century a certain Dr. James Graham, who essentially belonged to the type of Cagliostro, described, in his public lectures, various fantastic aphrodisiacal remedies. Richly and spaciously he exhorted his audience thus,

Suffer me, with great cordiality, and assurance of success, to recommend my celestial, or medico, magnetico, musico, electrical bed which I have constructed . . . to improve, exalt, and invigorate the bodily, and, through them, the mental faculties of the human species . . .

The sublime, the magnificent, and, I may say, the super-celestial dome of the bed, which contains the odoriferous, balmy, and ethereal spices, odors, and essences, and which is the grand magazine or reservoir of those vivifying and invigorating influences which are exhaled and dispersed by the breathing of the music, and by the attenuating, repelling, and accelerating force of the electrical fire—is very curiously inlaid or wholly covered on the under side with brilliant plates of looking-glass, so disposed as to reflect the various attractive charms of the happy recumbent couple, in the most flattering, most agreeable, and most enchanting style.

Such is a slight and inadequate sketch of the grand celestial bed, which, fully impregnated with the balmy vivifying effluvia of restorative balsamic medicines and of soft, fragrant, oriental gums, balsams, and quintessence, and pervaded at the same time with full springing tides of the invigorating influences of music and magnets both real and artificial, gives such elastic vigor to the nerves, on the one hand, of the male, and on the other, such retentive firmness to the female . . . that it is impossible, in the nature of things, but that strong, beautiful, brilliant, nay, double-distilled children, if I may use the expression, must infallibly be begotten.

Grape Juice
A drink that reputedly has aphrodisiac virtue.

Grapes
Believed to have amatory value.

Anciently, grapes were associated with the god Dionysus, deity of fertility and procreation.

Greek Comedy
Greek comedy, particularly in the case of the comic writer

Aristophanes, is permeated by the sex motif, dwelling on the supremacy of the phallus, erotic sexual practices, perversions, and orgies of a semi-religious nature.

In Aristophanes' *Acharnians*, for example, there is a glorification of the membrum virile in a phallus song.

In the *Ecclesiazusae*, a group of old and young prostitutes stage a singing match in alternating verse. One girl accuses another of singing in order to attract a lover. Another, decked out in grease paint and clad in a saffron-hued robe, hums an amatory melody to herself, to arouse a passer by.

Another, playing the flute, coaxes an ugly old fellow. A passing youth serenades one of the young girls.

Since sex was frankly without premeditation and as an ethnic characteristic accepted as a pervasive element of human life, and was accorded religious homage, comedy was not deliberately obscene, in the modern sense, when the comic actors appeared on the stage wearing a leathern phallus, to represent their service to Dionysus, the fertilizing god.

Grey
The learned and unfortunate Lady Jane Grey was accused of bewitching King Edward VI of England by means of strange potions and amatory charms.

Guinea Fowl
Roasted guinea fowl has been a favorite dish among French gourmets intent on sexual excitation.

H

Haleby, Omar

An Arab medical writer and sexologist who recommended the use of aphrodisiacs. This advice was in particular harmony with the practice in Islamic countries, permitting a muliplicity of wives, concubines, and slaves.

Halibut

This fish is considered to have stimulating aphrodisiac properties.

Hallucinations

The hallucinogenic drugs, though they may temporarily increase sexual awareness, may not necessarily promote amatory capacity.

Hallucinogens

A group of drugs that produce colorful visions and hallucinations, magnifying all forms of sensation. The drugs in this class may produce aphrodisiac effects by means of erotic visions and by the magnification of sensations. These visions occur with a marked sexual flavor, and an increased sensuality.

These drugs are derivatives of plants and may have aphrodisiac results, among them are yohombine, mescaline, nux vomica under certain conditions, rauwiloid, and brucine.

Handicaps to Potency

Among the conditions and sicknesses that are reputed to militate against amatory vigor are, nephritis, diabetes, tuberculosis of the lungs, obesity, poisoning by lead and mercury.

110

Hare Soup
The hare has a reputation for exciting desire. Hare soup is credited with a particular aphrodisiac value.

Haricot Beans
Considered to have stimulating aphrodisiac properties.

Harlotry at the Grave
The amatory licenses practised by public harlots were never in ancient Greece a matter of shame. On tombstones, for instance, were inscribed the careers and eulogies of such women. One such epitaph ran,

I was a harlot in the city of Byzantium . . .

I am Kallirrhoë, experienced in all the arts of voluptuousness.

Harmine
A drug chemically related to mescaline, dangerous.

See *MESCALINE*.

Harmine is obtained from the plant *banisteria caapi*. The plant grows in the foothills of the Andes and in the Amazon basin in South America. The leaves of the plant are used to make a greenish infusion that contains the alkaloid harmine. This alkaloid is also obtained from the seeds of the Wild Rue, which grows in Australia, New Zealand, and South America. Harmine is a drug that stimulates the brain and produces strange visual hallucinations, and also hallucinations of an erotic nature.

Harmless Aphrodisiacs
According to the Roman poet Ovid, author of the *Ars Amatoria,* aphrodisiacs that are harmless include eggs, honey, onions, wild cabbage, and stone-pine apples.

Hashish
An Indian hemp plant, *cannabis indica.* In Arabic = dried herb. It is chewed, smoked, and drunk. The term assassin is derived from the Arabic *hashishin, hemp eaters,* that is, drug addicts.

Among Moroccans, a popular aphrodisiac is a compound consisting of hashish, acorns, honey, sweet almonds, sesame, butter, cantharides, and nuts.

See *DRUGS*.

In its effects, hashish is demoralizing. It removes inhibitions and replaces them by emotional excitements. The sense of moral responsibility is lost, together with will power. The aphrodisiac effect stems from the creation of such excitement and the abandonment of restraints. The stimulation is local, occurring in the genitalia.

In the Orient, hashish is usually taken preceding sexual activity, but it is not a true aphrodisiac. Hallucinations and distortions of various kinds are accompanying effects.

In the case of marihuana, as inhibitions are removed, the smoker becomes highly suggestible and may incline toward sexual expression. Hence the reputation, though unwarranted, of marihuana as an aphrodisiac. The effect, if there is any, is very temporary and is due to this suggestibility. The addict actually becomes, in a short time, sexually inert. For this reason the hashish drug was used in the East to diminish sexual inclinations among monks and friars. Théophile Gautier, the nineteenth century French poet and novelist, was a hashish addict. He declared that "a hashish addict would not lift a finger for the most beautiful maiden in Verona."

Other notable men who have succumbed to the hashish habit were Gérard de Nerval, Honoré de Balzac, Alexandre Dumas and Charles Baudelaire in France, and Charles Lamb in England.

Hedysarum

For increasing vigor, an Oriental erotic text advises drinking the juices of hedysarum gangeticum, the kuli and the kshirika plants, in milk.

Hemlock

Hemlock is *conium maculatum*. In ancient times it was

a famous shrub widely used, but it is now practically obsolete. It grows in the hedges of Europe and is a member of the umbelliferae family. It has tall, smooth, hollow stalks, blue at the bottom and purplish at the top.

Conium comes from the Greek conos, a *top,* the allusion being to the giddiness of the head caused by hemlock.

In ancient times it had divine associations and was also used as a dreaded poison. Socrates, the Greek philosopher, was condemned to drink a cup of hemlock, from which he died, in 399 B.C.

Formerly hemlock was termed Herba Benedicta—*the blessed herb,* because "where the root is in the house the devil can do no harm, and if anyone should carry the plant about on his person, no venomous beast can harm him."

The Greek biographer Plutarch describes the medicinal properties of the herb and its poisonous effects.

As early as the tenth century the herb was used extensively in Anglo-Saxon medicine.

In the Tyrol, on May Day, it was the custom to smoke out witches by burning bundles of black and red spotted hemlock.

In the eighteenth century hemlock was used for treating cancer, syphilis, and ulcers.

Hemlock grows in the foothills of the Caucasus and in the Crimea. Being inert, the herb was eaten by cattle, but in other parts of Europe it is actively poisonous.

Mixed in a drink, hemlock was used anciently as a means of destroying virility.

Hemp

Among Turks, pills consisting of hemp buds, muscat nuts, saffron, and honey were a popular aphrodisiac. See *CANNABIS INDICA.*

Henbane

Also known as hyoscyamus, *bean of the hog.* Commonly called hogsbean. A drug is obtained from the flowering plant Hyoscyamus Niger, which grows in England and Europe. The plant has large, sea-green leaves and bell-shaped flowers, creamy-colored, streaked with purple, has a heavy, oppressive aroma, and is clammy to the touch.

Eaten by hogs and pigs, but a deadly poison for human beings.

Both Dioscorides and the Roman medical writer Celsus were familiar with henbane.

In France, the plant was called Jusquiame, in Germany it was known as the *Devil's Eye*.

In rural areas of Europe it was smoked like tobacco, but it produced convulsions and hallucinations.

Until recently henbane came from Egypt, and was known as Egyptian Henbane. In the Nile Delta it is called sakran, *the drunken.*

As a poison, there is warrant for believing that Shakespeare, in *Hamlet,* alludes to the drug,

> Sleeping within mine orchard,
> My custom always of the afternoon,
> Upon my secure hour thy uncle stole,
> With juice of cursed hebenon in a vial,
> And in the porches of mine ears did pour
> The leperous distilment.

Henbane acts as an anaphrodisiac.

Henna
The pulverized leaves and twigs of this plant are used as a hair-dye in European countries and the East. Among Arabs, it is believed that henna rubbed on the fingers, skull, and feet produces an aphrodisiac reaction.

Herbal Aphrodisiacs
In the sixteenth and seventeenth centuries herbals were compiled that listed traditionally known plants that were long reputed to have sex-provoking properties.

114

Herbal Massage

Petronius, the Roman novelist who wrote the *Satyricon*, describes a sexual massage involving a kind of cress and an aromatic herb known as southern-wood. The passage scarcely permits an English translation, but the Latin text runs as follows,

Nasturcii sucum cum habrotono miscet perfusisque inguinibus meis viridis urticae fascem comprehendit omniaque infra umbilicum coepit lenta manu caedere.

Herbs

Amongs herbs that have traditionally been considered to possess aphrodisiac virtue are, maidenhair, navelwort, anemone, wild poppy, valerian, cyclamen, male fern, pansy, periwinkle.

Herbs in Folklore

For hundreds of years, throughout all the continents, plants and herbs indigenous to particular regions have either been found to possess specific properties, or, through legend and folk customs, have been endowed with special qualities.

So it has been in the case of reputed aphrodisiac plants, seeds, oils, berries, leaves, sprouts, and juices.

In Bolivia and Peru, among the American Indians, in China, India, and in the Central European countries, as well as in the Mediterranean littoral, amatory virtues, the primary aim of man's probings, testings, and researches, have been attributed, sometimes erroneous, sometimes with startling validity, to such erotic aids.

Herissah

In the Orient, a concoction consisting of mutton and flour, seasoned with red pepper. Believed to be a sexual stimulant.

Hermes

In Greek cities the god Hermes was commemorated by the presence in public of numerous Hermes pillars. These were stone pillars surmounted by a head representing the god himself, and a phallus. A constant visual aphrodisiac reminder to *demos*.

Herring
Considered an aphrodisiac food.
This is the case with most species of fish.

Hesiod
In his *Works and Days*, this ancient Greek poet says that in summer "women are then most lascivious, but men are most impotent."

Hierodouloi
Sexual indulgence was, in ancient Greece, virtually a religious duty consistent with the worship of Aphrodite, goddess of love. Hence it is easy to appreciate the religious status of the hierodouloi, the sacred temple prostitutes.

Such temple slaves were known to many cults in various countries, to the Egyptians and to the people of Asia Minor.

In the religious cults of the Orient the same practice was prevalent, especially in India.

See *The Temple Girls of India, Fate*, vol. I, no. 3, pages 58-60.

The temple of Aphrodite of Byblos in Phoenicia was noted for its hierodouloi. So too with the cult of Mylitta in Babylonia.

In Cyprus, at Amathos and Paphos, the hierodouloi of the temples were dedicated to Aphrodite Astarte. Among the Romans, in the temple of Venus Erycina on Mount Eryx in Sicily, the hierodouloi had a widespread reputation.

The sacred prostitute was equally an institution in ancient Semitic times. The prostitute was known as a q'deshah.

Reference to the custom occurs in the Bible,

Now Eli was very old, and heard all that his sons did unto all Israel; and how they lay with the women

116

PLATE 7—Casanova de Seingalt by Giacomo Girolamo (1725-98)
(from an old print)
Casanova, here represented in one of his numerous amorous adventures,
is the supreme type of the traditional lover.

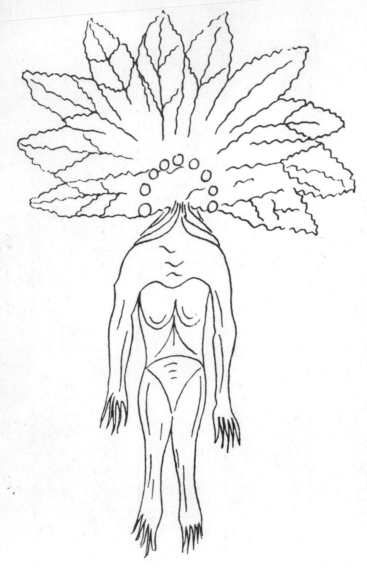

PLATE 8—Mandrake (Female)
(From a manuscript of the fourteenth century in the British
Museum)

that assembled of the door of the tabernacle of the congregation.

I Samuel 2.22

Again,

But all the women children, that have not known a man by lying with him, keep alive for yourselves.

And thirty and two thousand persons in all, of women that had not known man by lying with him.

Numbers 31. 18, 35

In Babylonia, in the Temple of Bit-Shagatha, The Place of Union, every female, once in her life, had to practice the sacred act of prostitution with a stranger.

Hieronymus

Hieronymus of Rhodes, a philosopher of the third century B.C., author of *Historical Memoirs,* filled with erotic episodes.

Hindu Advice

A well-known Hindu erotic manual, in spite of its forthrightness, makes serious recommendations that would seem to be somewhat inconsistent with the apparently, but only apparently, lascivious nature of the text.

The means of producing sexual vigor, it asserts, should be learned from reputable medical men, from the sacred Vedas, and, it adds, from magicians skilled in occult love and from close relatives. No means should be tried which are doubtful in their effects, or likely to cause bodily injury, or involving the death of animals, or associated with contacts with impure things.

Hindu Aphrodisiacs

Onions, beans, garlic, leeks are constantly mentioned as conducive to sexual activity, also in epic literature, the eating of flesh. Heady drinks, festivals enlivened with music likewise promote erotic designs. Among the recommended

117

drinks are madhirka, extracted from flowers, and madhu-madhavi, made from honey.

The natural beauties too are listed as love inspirers, the wind in spring time, the humming of bees, flowers budding, the songs of birds.

Athenaeus, an old Greek encyclopedist, quoting an ancient historian, says that some Indian aphrodisiacs were so powerful that, applied to the soles of the feet, they immediately increased passion.

Hindu Charms

In the Hindu love manuals, special chapters are devoted to charms and drugs intended to attract and retain love, as well as recipes whose purpose was to achieve complete mastery over the person loved.

Hindu Courtesans

The Kama Sutra, the Hindu erotic manual, classifies courtesans thus, female attendants, unchaste women, bawds, dancing girls, female artisans, women who have left their family, women living on their beauty, regular courtesans.

Evidently, these names overlap, and the classification is no more rigid than the multiple names applied to the harlots of ancient Rome.

Hindu Ideal

In some respects, Hindu ideals of feminine perfection coincide with those of Arab countries. The face should be as pleasing as the new moon. The body should be soft as the mustard flower. A fine, fair, tender skin is a requisite. Eyes bright as those of a fawn. Bosom full and firm. The nose straight. A swan-like gliding gait. The voice low and musical, while the garments should be white, flowing, adorned with jewels.

Hindu Love Manuals

India is rich in erotic literature, written originally in

Sanskrit, and later on translated into various vernacular languages, notably Hindi.

These texts are as follows,

The Ratirahasya, The Secrets of Love, by the poet Kukoka. Translated into Hindi.

The Panchasakya, The Five Arrows, by the poet Jyotirisha. Comprises some 600 verses.

The Rasmanjari, The Sprout of Love, by the poet Bhanudatta.

The Smara Pradipa, The Light of Love, by the poet Gunakara. Comprises 400 verses.

The Ratimanjari, The Garland of Love, by the poet Jayadeva.

Hindu Ointment

An aphrodisiac ointment, recommended by the *Kama Sutra,* the Hindu erotic manual, runs as follows,

Tabernamontana coronaria, xanthochymus pichorius, ghee and honey, blue lotus, mesna roxburghii, nelumbrium speciosum.

Hindu Passion

In Hindu tradition, sexual excitement is induced by touch, aromas, sound, taste, and form.

Hindu Powder

An amatory enticement is as follows, according to a famous erotic manual,

Eating the powder of the nelumbrium speciosum, the blue lotus, and the mesna roxburghii, with ghee and honey.

Hindu Recipe

Ointments and powders made from the plants known botanically as tabernamontana coronaria, costus speciosus, and flacourtia cataphracta, are said to heighten physical appeal and induce sexual provocation.

119

Hippocras Aphrodisiac

According to folk tradition, a potent sexual stimulant. It consits of red Burgundy wine with an admixture of ginger, crushed cinnamon, cloves, vanilla, and white sugar. Rabelais, in *Gargantua and Pantagruel*, refers to its healthful value,

Then shall you be presented with a cup of claret hypocras, which is right healthful and stomachal.

Hippocrates

Hippocrates, the most famous Greek physician, who died in the same year as Socrates, in 399 B.C., declared that a predisposing cause of impotence among the ancient Scythians was the wearing of breeches. Arab erotologists express similar views about more modern conditions.

Hippomanes

A protuberance that appears on a colt's head at birth and that is bitten off by the mare. Hippomanes was used in ancient Roman potions as an aphrodisiac. It was as large as a fig, black in color, and derived its name from a Greek expression meaning *horse-madness*.

Vergil, Ovid, Pliny the Elder, Juvenal all describe hippomanes as an excrescence on a new-born colt. In the *Aeneid*, Vergil, listing the operations of a witch-priestess, says, She has sprinkled water, so she feigns, from Avernus' spring and she is getting green downy herbs cropped by moonlight with brazen shears, whose sap is the milk of deadly poison, and the love-charm, torn from the brow of the new-born foal, ere the mother could snatch it.

Another meaning of hippomanes occurs in the same poet, in his *Georgics*,

Then it is there trickles from the mares a thick fluid, which the shepherds rightly call hippomanes, which fell step-dames have oft gathered up, to form a mess with herbs and charms as baleful.

Pausanias, a Greek traveler, has likewise something to say of hippomanes,

one of these horses the Aelians declare to have been
made by a magician, of brass, into which metal he had
previously infused the hippomanes . . . which possessed
the power of exciting horses to a mad desire for coition.
An old dramatist says,

Then hippomanes, for shepheards call it so,
Distil as venom from their parts below,
Hippomanes that wicked stepdames pluck,
Mingling with herbs that bring bad luck.

Homosexual Festival

In the first century B.C., in ancient Rome, a special
festival, dedicated to this perversion, was celebrated annually
on April 23.

Homosexuality

In Greek mythology, homosexuality is a common theme,
just as it was a recognized practice in actual Greek life. Of
the god Apollo it was related that he had twenty male
favorites.

Honey

In Oriental dishes intended as aphrodisiacs, honey is a
frequent ingredient.

Galen, a Greek of the second century A.D., court physician to the Emperor Marcus Aurelius, recommended as an
effective aphrodisiac a glass of thick honey, taken before
bedtime, together with the consumption of almonds and
one hundred grains of the pine tree. The recipe was to be
followed for three successive days.

A compound of honey, pepper, and ginger is recommended as an aphrodisiac by the thirteenth century Arab
physician Avicenna.

Horseradish

As a condiment, reputed to have a stimulating sexual
value.

Hydromel

A beverage consisting of honey and water. Once taken as an aphrodisiac.

Hypnosis

Hypnosis and auto-suggestive methods have been used in the treatment of persons affected by sexual conditions, especially as a means of encouraging amatory expression. Hypnosis, however, should never be resorted to without rigid and authoritative medical control.

Ibogene

A drug obtained from a plant known as *ibogo, tabenanthe,* or *cheha edulis.* It is indigenous to the Yemen, in Arabia. Ibogene is markedly anti-sexual in its effects.

Certain native tribes use it as a beverage.

Incapacity Described in Juvenal

The Roman satirist Juvenal forcefully describes this condition,

vel si

Coneris, iacet exiguus cum ramice nervus,
Et, quamvis tota palpetur nocte, iacebit.

Indian Plant

Venette recounts that a certain *herb of Theophrastus* was sent as a gift to King Antiochus. It was reputed to act as a powerful aphrodisiac.

See *VENETTE.*

Indian Root

A Greek historian Phylarchus describes a white root indigenous to India that caused eunuchism when a person bathed in water in which the root was steeped.

See *PHYLARCHUS.*

Ineffectiveness of Anti-Aphrodisiacs

The potency of some aphrodisiacs, whether philtres or incantations or other magic rites, was apparently so great, so universally known and accepted, that it appeared futile to combat them. So the Roman poet Tibullus, in the first cen-

tury B.C., laments his inability to throw off his passion by
anti-aphrodisiac means,

What shall I believe? For she said that she could free
me from this passion by her spells and herbs.

So too a later Roman poet, Nemesianus, who belongs in
the third century A.D., cries,

What avails it that Amynta purified me thrice with fillets,
thrice with the sacred leaf, and thrice with incense, and
averting her face threw ashes into the stream, burning the
crackling laurels with live sulphur, when in my miserable
plight I was all on fire with love for Meroe?

Influence of the Seasons

The seasons of the year, and the temperature, subtly
influence amorous desires. Hesiod, an ancient Greek poet,
author of *Work and Days*, dwells on the time "When the
artichoke flowers and the chirping cicada, perched upon a
tree, pours down its shrill song continuously from beneath its
wings in the season of tiring summer, then kids are fattest,
and wine is most mellow, and women are most lustful, but
men are feeblest, for the skin is dry through the heat."

This feeble condition of the male, however, may soon be
remedied, declares the poet, by a good meal fortified by
wine.

Internal Organs

The liver and the kidneys of animals have long been
gastronomically popular for their aphrodisiac properties.

Interpretation of Dreams

Nefzawi, rather ingenuously, offers numerous fantastic
explanations and interpretations of dream sequences in *The
Perfumed Garden*. In some cases, on the other hand, he seems
to coincide with Freudian psychology.

Many of his interpretations are illustrated with pertinent
anecdotes and legends and folktales that involve sexual
symbolism.

See *PERFUMED GARDEN*.

124

Intestines

The intestines of fish and birds were used as aphrodisiacs among the Romans.

Italian Plant

In Italy, a plant called *Pizza ugurdu* is said to excite powerful erotic feelings even in the most frigid. It has been identified with the Greek *Vorax*.

Italian Soup

An Italian soup recipe, described as of aphrodisiac virtue, contains, calves' heel, crayfish, carrots, celery, and shallots.

Italian Stimuli

In a manual of erotic cookery, among ingredients that tend toward amatory expression are listed, basil, snakeroot, soup seasoned with cloves, laurel, truffles, celery, thyme, parsley, fennel, artichoke, chocolate.

It may be noted that certain foods, herbs, beverages recur consistently in the accumulations of aphrodisiac material gathered through the centuries and in every continent. Manifestly, the properties of pepper, truffles, various other roots and herbs, have demonstrated such aphrodisiac virtues as to warrant their inclusion in the stream of folklore and even in the more literate acceptances.

Ithyphallus

One of the major and still unattained quests in the erotic field is a means of effecting an ithyphallic condition for the proper physiological functioning of amatory practices.

All kinds of bizarre and complicated preparations have been concocted in various countries and in various centuries. Some of these compounds are innocuous and ineffective, others are harmful and involve dangerous hazards. Historically, they all have a certain academic interest. These preparations include oils, powders, brews, unguents, not to mention electuaries, mechanical contrivances, charms, incantations, and occult supplications. Through the ages, from ancient Greek centuries down to contemporary days, and in every habitable region, in the Orient and the Middle East, in primitive tribal communities in the Pacific Islands, in the South American continent, and in the vast stretches of Asia, legends and oral traditions have accumulated and have been preserved. What then was the efficacious key to the achievement and maintenance of the priapic virtue?

The sources that putatively offered guidance and counsel, if not specific recipes and directives for this purpose, include the secrets of witchcraft, folk legends, the concentrated knowledge of tested tribal experimentation, together with the grimoires of professional sorcerers, the fantastic directions of alchemists and astrologers, herbalists and charlatans, pseudo mystics and adventurers. Later on, in the Middle Ages, medical knowledge advanced to such an extent that textbooks on materia medica and germane subjects often treated this area of erotica. Professors of medicine in the Italian universities, such as Sinibaldus, practicing physicians in France, such as the learned Dr. Venette, on occasion roués and amorous adventurers, such as Cagliostro and Casanova, experienced in erotic contacts, revealed secrets that were hitherto the subjects only of subdued whispers of cryptic counsel.

In the Orient, on the other hand, the entire subject of amorous relationships, the difficulties attendant on senescence and decay, the conflicts between men and women of varying temperaments, the aberrations and perversions of men, and even the questions arising from the practices of public and commercialized amatory expression all received sober, lengthy, detailed consideration. All the love manuals of the East, therefore, examine this subject without suggestive innuendoes, without primness or repressions, but with an open mind, in a mature and serious spirit, as a factor in human attitudes, adequate human relationships, competent social and domestic functioning. There is even, in the Arab manuals in particular, a reverent tone, free from priggishness, that in-

126

cludes all physiological activities as a phase of the divine design, and frees the subject from frustrations, and from shamed secretiveness, and also from suggestions of lubricity.

The Oriental manuals, notably the Arab, Chinese, and Hindu guides, offer extensive, elaborate direction for ithyphallic consummations. Travelers and anthropologists, too, have made additional contributions. A certain Dr. Jacobus, a French army surgeon, in a rather rare book entitled *Untrodden Fields of Anthropology*, discusses the subject with frankness and precision. Sir Richard Burton, the Orientalist and traveler, in his translations from Asiatic sources, and particularly in his commentaries and notes stemming from his personal acquaintance, both wide and unique, of the Orient and its mores, brought the subject into public awareness. Anthropological studies, in fact, have in many cases illuminated traditional obscurities and have presented, pari passu, as much enlightening information, factual and tested, on erotic situations as numberless academic or systematic accounts.

Specifically, the recommendations that appear in the anthropological studies, the erotic manuals, and various commentaries and monographs, include concoctions for internal use, massage treatments, manipulative devices, herbal and similar applications, even surgical operations. Sometimes the Eastern herbs and berries, the exotic ointments, animal secretions, juices and electuaries, together with the recommended brews and elixirs, are difficult to secure. In other cases, the recommendations involve grave hazards, both emotional and physiological.

J

Jacobus

The identity of Dr. Jacobus X, author of the remarkable *Untrodden Fields of Anthropology*, is still somewhat of an enigma. The New York Academy of Medicine makes, under the name, the following comments,

The identity of this author has not been definitely clarified. According to Esar Levine (*Chastity Belts*, N.Y. 19–) this author's true name was Dr. Jacobus Sutor. Mr. Levine's authority for this statement is a reference in *The Secrets of Woman*, Paris, 1899. The original Jacobus X's work, *L'Amour aux Colonies*, Paris 1893, seems to be the posthumous work of Dr. Louis Jacolliot, who had been a French army-surgeon in just the countries treated of in the work, and whose literary style in his innumerable works—if literary style is valid internal evidence—very closely corresponds to that of Jacobus X. *L'Amour aux Colonies* was published in Paris by Charles Carrington in 1896 and was reissued, enlarged, by Carrington, in 1898.

According to those who hold to the Dr. Jacobus Sutor attribution, both *L'Amour aux Colonies* and all the later Jacobus X's works were written by this Sutor. However, since none of the later Jacobus X's works are translations from the French, but are original English works, a more plausible theory is that Carrington wished to make the most of the financial success of *Untrodden Fields of Anthropology,* the English translation of *L'Amour aux Colonies,* and either himself wrote, or had written for him, a whole series of books purporting to be by the same Dr. Jacobus X, but actually almost certainly by some one other than the author of *L'Amour aux Colonies.*

In his professional career as an army surgeon, Dr. Jacobus traveled through many countries, East and West. He is familiar with the United States, Cochin-China, Africa and Oceania, Guiana and Tonkin, Cambodia and the West Indies.

Janus
Several centuries ago a certain Madame Janus gained in Paris and throughout France a notorious and sinister reputation in connection with Shunammitism. Under her supervision she had some forty girls whom she hired out to clients as shunammites.

See *SHUNAMMITISM*.

Jealousy
Jealousy has been considered as an indirect sexual stimulant.

In one of the Greek satirist Lucian's *Dialogues of Courtesans,* a conversation takes place between the hetaira Tryphaena and a young client named Charmides. Tryphaena arouses the visitor to a frenzied pitch of amorous activity by describing the faded realities of Charmides' previous object of passion, a certain Philemation.

Juniper
A shrub that produces fleshly berries, of purple color and pungent taste. Yields an oil used medicinally. The berries are steeped in water and the juice is drunk. John Gerarde, author of *Herball*, 1633, recommends it as a wholesome drink. Juniper is also credited with the virtue of maintaining youthful ardor.

A shrub used as an ingredient in cordials. Formerly juniper was considered of medicinal value by herbalists. It was also used in love philtres.

Juno Virginensis
Among the Romans, this was the goddess who presided over the consummation of marriage.

Juvenal

In connection with the sexual excesses of Roman matrons, Juvenal, the Roman satirist who lived in the second century A.D., makes a reference to hippomanes,

Shall I speak of hippomanes, and incantations, and poisonous concoctions?

See *HIPPOMANES*.

K

Kallipygian Coquetry

Amorous provocation by the sensuous kallipygian movements of girls and wives is a theme elaborated by the old Greek poet Hesiod. He gives a warning against this type of allurement as coquettish and vain.

Kalogynomia

The Laws of Female Beauty. A book on love techniques, rules of intercourse, prostitution, infidelity, together with a catalogue of female defects. Published in London, in 1821. The author was a certain Dr. T. Bell.

An early comprehensive text in English dealing with sexological subjects.

Kama

A Sanskrit term used to express sexual pleasure, a motivating force in Hindu life.

Kama Sutra

A Sanskrit manual of erotic procedures.

Written by Vatsyayana. This comprehensive vade mecum has been translated into English by Sir Richard Burton the Orientalist.

In addition to offering specific formulas and prescriptions for inducing amatory excitement, the Kama Sutra advises, in regard to sexual problems, consultation with family elders and relatives, the reading of the Sanskrit Vedas, visits to physicians and magicians.

It is also forthright in warning against injurious and impure concoctions, and items that are destructive of animal life. Only such objects should be used as are known to be beneficial and acceptable to Brahmans.

Kama Sutra itself means *Aphorisms on Love*. There are some twelve hundred verses, ranging in great detail over all amatory topics, and dwelling particularly on aphrodisiac aids.

All the directions and counsel given in the Kama Sutra stress that the prudent, intelligent man will, instead of enslaving himself to passion, succeed in mastering his senses.

Kantaka

The *Kama Sutra,* the most expressive and detailed erotic manual, originally composed in Sanskrit, suggests, as a means of increasing vigor, a mixture that is to be thrown at the woman in question. The mixture consists of powder of milk hedge plant and kantaka plant, together with monkey excrement and the powdered root of the lanjalika plant.

Karengro

A gypsy term meaning *boy-plant*. Found in Transylvania. It has some resemblance to an orchid, and is believed to promote conception.

Kava Piperaceae

A plant found in the entire area of the South Sea Islands. The roots produce a liqueur called kava. Kava has a mild aphrodisiac effect. The Polynesian natives drink kava after wedding ceremonies and are evidently stimulated by the drink.

Kava drink is made by chewing the root of the pepper plant and spitting it into a kava bowl. The drink is then strained and served in a coconut cup.

Kidneys

The kidneys of sheep, pigs, and cattle are believed to stimulate the sexual functions.

King's Crow

In Malaya, a love philtre is made with the bile of a bird called King's Crow.

Kissing

Kissing is essentially a sexual act. It is the introductory phase that creates an intimacy often resulting in sexual consummation.

That is the view of Ovid, the Roman poet who produced the *Ars Amatoria*. He declares that the man who has stolen a kiss and does not know how to steal the rest deserves to lose his advantage.

The kissing of lips, tongue, and other parts of the body is basically an erotic caress and acts as a sexual stimulant to those so engaged.

Kitab Al-Izah Fi'ilm Al-Nikah

A famous Arabic manual on sexual operations, aphrodisiacs, and similar erotic topics. Written by the Arab historian Jalai al-Din al-Siyuti. An English translation was published at the beginning of this century in Paris.

Kite

In Hindu erotic literature, to consummate sexual supremacy, a prescription often in use requires a mixture of honey and cowach, the prickly hairs of a tropical pod, along with the remains of a dead kite, in pulverized form.

Koran

Nefzawi, expatiating on amatory themes in *The Perfumed Garden*, alludes to the Koran. He asserts,

It is said that reading the Koran also predisposes for copulation.

See *PERFUMED GARDEN*.

Kosth

In the Hindu amatory tradition, comprehensively illustrated in the *Ananga-Ranga,* sexual power is increased by the following means,

Kosth, which is costus arabicus, lechi, chikana, askhand, kanher root, gajapimpali, pounded and mixed with butter. The compound is applied to the genitals.

Most of the ingredients are indigenous to India.

Kshemendra

Hindu author of Samayamatrika, a description of a harlot's progress. It contains lists of aphrodisiacs, including the usual beans, leeks, onions, garlic.

Kuili

To recover sexual vigor, the Hindu manual *Ananga-Ranga* directs as follows,

Kuili powder, Kanta-gokhru, lechi, asparagus racemosus, and cucumber. Mixed with milk, the resultant drink is highly strengthening.

Most of the above ingredients are indigenous to India.

Kuttanimatam

A Hindu manual on sexual techniques, by Damodaragupta. Has been translated into French and English.

Kyphi

An ancient Egyptian compound applied to the genitals to arouse sexual desire.

L

L'ami De Bacchus
An early nineteenth century collection of French songs intended to be a stimulant at table festivities.

See *SONGS*.

L'ami De La Joie
A collection of French songs, published in 1806, and intended for convivial occasions.

See *SONGS*.

Lamprey
This eel-like pseudo-fish is said to increase the seminal fluid.

Lampsacus
A city in Asia Minor, noted for its obscene rites associated with Priapus.

It is mentioned in this connection by the Roman erotic poet Catullus.

See *PRIAPUS*.

Lao-Tze
A famous Chinese philosopher who flourished in the seventh century B.C. He was noted for his quest of rejuvenating processes.

Lard
Lard mixed with crushed and strained garlic has been used as an erotic ointment.

La Siang Koeng
A Chinese expression meaning *The Great Lord*. Also

known as Kak Ishia—Chariot of Horn. An instrument of soft leather or thin horn, stuffed with cotton, and used in the East for perverted amatory purposes.

Latin Apothegm

A Latin apothegm on love runs as follows,
Dulce balneum suavibus
unguentatum odoribus
A delightful bath anointed with subtle perfumes.

Laurel Leaves

Laurel leaves were used in the Orient to promote amatory exercise.

Lavender

Small doses of lavender are said to cause excitation. A few flowers in tobacco induce a dream-like state.

Le Chansonnier Bachique De L'Amour Et De La Folie

A collection of French songs intended for banquets, weddings and similar occasions. Published by a society of gourmets in Paris, in 1816. They created the proper convivial and erotic atmosphere. Since antiquity, especially among the Greeks and the Romans, obscenities, lubricities, erotic activity have been associated with the sense of euphoria stimulated by gastronomic plenitude and diversions.

Lecithin

This nitrogenous fatty substance that appears in certain foods is considered an element in inducing sexual desire.

Lentils

In ancient Greece, lentils were believed to stimulate desire.

Lesbianism

The fact of Lesbianism has been common knowledge

since remote antiquity. As subject matter for fictional treatment, the following titles may here be mentioned,

Diderot's *La Religieuse,*
Honoré de Balzac's *La Fille aux Yeux d'Or,*
Théophile Gautier's *Mademoiselle de Maupin,*
Sacher-Masoch, *Venus im Pelz,*
Butti, *L'Automna.*

Libya

In ancient times, the Romans imported truffles, credited with marked aphrodisiac virtue, from Libya as well as Greece.

Liébault, Jean

(c. 1535-1596). A French sexologist, native of Dijon and member of the Faculty of Medicine in Paris. Author of *Thrésor des Remèdes Secrets pour Les Maladies des Femmes.* It was originally written in Latin by Liébault, who translated it into French in 1582.

It is an encyclopedia of sexual knowledge as it was known in his time.

He makes detailed suggestions on the means of strengthening sexual vigor, analyzing conditions as organic or psychological, and advising in accordance with each specific condition. In a general sense, he recommends, as a stimulus, sound and wholesome, proper diet, special foods, drinks, along with electuaries and ointments, massage and similar exercises whose purpose is to reinforce the erotic feelings and tendencies. He enumerates, in a long list of recipes and prescriptions, diasatyrion and dates, nuts, figs, wine in moderation, ointments applied to the body, game, fresh fish cooked in onions, pomegranates. A warm bath is a pleasant stimulant, to be followed by a period of sleep. Chestnuts are advisable, also chicken soup, mutton, lamb, veal prepared in special ways, fatted suckling pigs. Most dishes have their own sauces. Spices in great variety are listed, cardamom, long pepper, ginger, cubebs, saffron, cinnamon, galanga. These spices may be used on meats and in pastry. Rice cooked in milk of sheep is advised as a potent aid. Also certain pharmaceutical items that were in common use in the seventeenth century.

In addition, beyond all mechanical, gastronomic, and external aids, there should be amatory talk, erotic thoughts, exercise in the peripheral erotic advances, as well as tactile contacts. All these procedures, Liébault advises, should, cumulatively, produce the desired consummations.

Lingam Preparations

In the famous Hindu guide to erotology, the Ananga-Ranga, in respect of phallic effectiveness, applications are advised that include, anise, honey, leaves of the jai, rui seed, Hungarian grass, and lotus flower pollen.

Liniments

A seventeenth century erotologist lists, among unguents and liniments that have active sexual impact, the following ingredients,

honey, goose fat, butter, storax, ghee, spurge, chives, musk, ginger, ambergris, pepper.

Lion's Fat

Sinibaldus lists lion's fat as a popular medieval aphrodisiac treatment.

See *GENEANTHROPOEIA*.

Liqueurs

Many liqueurs, among them chartreuse and benedictine, have long been held in great esteem as aphrodisiac aids.

Liquids

Nefzawi, the author of the erotic manual entitled *The Perfumed Garden,* asserts that greasy liquids act as an anti-aphrodisiac.

See *PERFUMED GARDEN*.

Liver

According to the Roman poet Horace, liver was popular in his days as an aphrodisiac.

Lizard

Lizards are favored in Arab countries for their reputed erotic stimulus.

An Arab recipe for potency consists of Chinese cubebs, cloves, cinnamon, Roumi opium, ginger, cardamom, mountain lizard, and white pepper. Pounded together, and boiled in sweet olive oil. Male frankincense is added, and coriander seed. The entire composition is now macerated and mixed with bee honey. Taken after supper, washed down with rose conserve sherbet.

By itself, the lizard is powdered and drunk with sweet wine, acting as an aphrodisiac. When held in the hand, the lizard produces an amorous stimulus.

Localized Perfumes

Among the Arabs, who are highly sensitive to aromas as sexual stimulants, perfume is applied for this purpose to the mouth, the armpits, nasally, and the *pudenda muliebria*.

Loha-Bhasma

A preparation of ferrous oxide, used in India as an aphrodisiac.

Love and Be Loved

Basically, according to some authorities on sexology and related fields, the most effective, the most natural aphrodisiac is the passion itself for the object of love. That passion, intense and prolonged, should be sufficient, under normal conditions, they assert, to achieve all necessary amatory consummations.

Ovid, the experienced ancient authority in this sphere, the author of several long amatory poems, notably the *Ars Amatoria*, which is virtually the manual of love *par ex-*

139

cellence throughout all Western Europe, says, To be loved, be lovable.

This definitive, succinct injunction is repeated at later times. Seneca, the philosopher and dramatist, declares,

I shall show you a philtre without potions, without herbs, without any witch's incantation—If you wish to be loved, love.

Martial, the epigrammatist, gives identical advice to a friend,

If you want to be loved, Marcus, love.

Love Charm

Such devices have always been popular, particularly in the Orient. In India, women use a variety of charms and amulets to inspire or retain passion in their lovers.

See *CHARMS*.

Love Feast

On the island of Cyprus the birth and first manifestation of the goddess Aphrodite were elaborated into a celebration at which all the people gathered. The goddess' image was bathed in the sea by women and girls, then decked with garlands. Bathing in the river followed, culminating in love orgies, the preceding formalities being in a sense introductory stimulants.

Love For Sale

Quacks and herbalists, alchemists and occultists, in Europe as well as in China, in the Amazon valley no less than in Himalayan retreats, have through the centuries offered, frequently as a mere tantalizing but provocative illusion, certainty of sexual capacity and pleasure by means of spells and invocations, drugs and periapts, brews and unguents and weird physical administrations.

Love Incantations

Pindar, the Greek poet who belongs in the fifth century

B.C., asserts that Aphrodite, the goddess of love, taught the lore of suppliant incantations.

This was achieved by means of the iynx, the wry-neck or woodpecker. This bird's neck shimmers with the play of color, and in a sense reflected the frantic, restless movements of love itself. The bird was stretched upon a four-spoked colored wheel, its feet and wings being tied, then the wheel was whirled round rapidly.

Love Nests

In ancient Greece, at Cnidus and Olympia and elsewhere, there were pandokeia, *inns,* that ostensibly constituted shelters for visitors and travelers but in practice were haunts for sexual enjoyments.

Greek inns, in general, were frequently managed by women, who often used their premises as brothels.

Theophrastus, a Greek philosopher of the third century B.C., considers inns and brothels synonymous.

Love Romances

Among a number of Greek erotic tales that have come down to us are the story of Chaereas and Kallirrhoe, by Chariton who lived in the second century A.D., and the love of Abrocomes and Antheia, by Xenophon of Ephesus. Heliodorus of Emesa produced the story of Theagenes and Chariclea. Longus of Lesbos is the author of the romance of Daphnis and Chloe.

Lozenges

Anciently, lozenges and pastilles, perfumed with ambergris, were on sale as aphrodisiac aids. They were called, appropriately enough, avunculae Cypriae—the Aunts of the Cyprian goddess (Venus).

Lust

St. Augustine, who flourished in the fifth century A.D., admits the intense sexual urges of men. If you banish prosti-

141

tutes from society, he declares, you reduce society to chaos through unsatisfied lust.

Lycopodium
A plant with a claw-like root, once believed to have aphrodisiac properties.

Lysergic Acid, Diethyl-Amide, Adrenochrome
These drugs are similar in action to mescaline.
See *MESCALINE*.

These drugs produce hallucinations and may have erotic features, but they are highly dangerous and should not be used without proper medical consultation.

M

Macaronic Verse

A macaronic epigram, in both Latin and English, illustrates the reputed amorousness and perversions of medieval monks,

Let a friar of some order tecum pernoctare,
Either thy wife or thy daughter hic vult violare,
Or thy son he will prefer, sicut fortem fortis,
God, give such a friar pain in Inferni portis.

Machon

Machon of Sicyon, a Greek poet of the third century B.C. Author of *Chreiae*, a miscellany covering scandalous and erotic anecdotes, particularly about the hetairae.

Mackerel

Believed to stimulate amatory desire.
This is the case with most species of fish.

Maerua Arenaria

A herb native to India, used to promote sexual vigor.

Magical Remedies

In the late seventeenth century concoctions, intended for aphrodisiac purposes and involving scatological ingredients, were officially endorsed by the University Faculty of Leipzig, in Germany.

Magic Pharmacopoeia

In the Middle Ages, among occult practitioners there was a kind of standardized and acknowledged pharmacopoeia whose aim was the furtherance of erotic capacity.

Male Prostitution

This practice was familiar in Biblical times,

And he brake down the houses of the sodomites, that were by the houses of the Lord, where the women wove hangings for the grove.

2 Kings 23.7.

Also,

They die in youth and their life is among the unclean.

Job 36.14.

Mallows

The root of mallow in goat's milk excites the sexual urge, according to Pliny the Elder, the Roman encyclopedist of the first century A.D. If the root was eaten dry, on the other hand, it was believed to act as an anti-aphrodisiac.

The sap of mallows, together with three mallow roots tied together, aroused the passions of woman, according to the same writer.

Mandrake

This plant, also called mandragore, is the *atropa mandragora, mandragora officinarum,* and belongs to the potato family. It has dark leaves, with purple flowers, and a tomato-like fruit, and is indigenous to the Mediterranean area, especially Palestine. The Hebrew name for mandrakes is *dudaim,* from the root *dud,* meaning *love.* Pharmaceutically tested in recent times, mandrake shows aphrodisiac properties.

It often grows in human shape, taking the form of limbs. Mandrake was regularly used in the preparation of love philtres. The ancient Homeric witch Circe used infusions of it in her magic brews, hence the root was also known as "the plant of Circe."

The erotic effectiveness of mandrake is illustrated in Genesis 30. 14-16,

And Reuben, going out in the time of the wheat harvest into the field, found mandrakes, which he brought to his mother Leah. And Rachel said,

Give me part of thy son's mandrakes.

She answered, Dost thou think it a small matter, that

144

thou hast taken my husband from me, unless thou take also my son's mandrakes?

Rachel said, He shall sleep with thee this night, for thy son's mandrakes.

And when Jacob returned at even from the field, Leah went out to meet him, and said, Thou shalt come in unto me, because I have hired thee for my son's mandrakes. And he slept with her that night.

In the eighteenth century Chinese mandragora was the name for ginseng.

A mandragorite was a term applied to one addicted to mandrake as a narcotic.

Shakespeare uses the expression in this sense,

> Not poppy, nor mandragora,
> Nor all the drowsy syrups of the world
> Shall ever medicine thee to that sweet sleep
> Which thou owd'st yesterday.
>
> *Othello* 3.3.330

In folklore, the eating of mandrake is considered an aid in conception.

In the Middle Ages mandrake was regularly used in magic rites and in sorcery.

In the *Song of Solomon* 7.14 there is a reference to the mandrake,

"The mandrakes give a smell and at our gates are all manner of pleasant fruits, new and old, which I have laid up for thee, O my beloved."

The Greek biographer Plutarch called the plant "man-likeness," because it sometimes resembles the human form and sometimes the testes and the membrum virile. The Roman encyclopedist, Pliny the Elder, says in his *Natural History*. It is said to bear a marked likeness to the genitals of either sex; it is rarely met with, but if a root resembling the male organ of the human species is found by a man, it will ensure him woman's love.

Columella, a Roman poet, calls mandrake *semi-human*.

145

The Arabs call it *face of an idol* or *man-plant*. In Germany it was called *The Little Gallows Man*. This term is associated with the folk tradition that mandrakes sprang up in ground near which a criminal had been hanged on a gallows.

The yellow fruit of the mandrake, of the size of large plums, emits a peculiar, characteristic odor.

A seventeenth century traveler says that the eating of mandrake helps conception. The Greeks used the root, to excite passion. Hence the association with the goddess Aphrodite, who was known as Mandragoritis, *She of the Mandrake*.

In contemporary Greece the amatory properties of mandrake are still credited. Late in the nineteenth century, in Athens, young men carried pieces of mandrake with them in their satchels as love-charms. So in Italy, too, the comedy *Mandragola* was based on the power of the mandrake to make women fruitful.

John Gerarde, author of *The Herball or General Historie of Plantes*, published in 1633, talks of the beneficial effect of the plant on barren women. He also adds,

There have been many ridiculous tales brought up of this plant, whether of old wives, or some runnagate surgeons, or physicke-mongers I know not, but sure some one or more that sought to make themselves famous or skilful above others were the first brocher of that errour I speak of . . . Besides many fables of loving matters, too full of scurrilitie to set forth in print, which I forbeare to speak of.

Sir James G. Frazer, in his *Folk Lore in the Old Testament*, say that orthodox Jews in America imported, as late as the latter decades of the nineteenth century, mandrake from the Orient for barren wives.

In folklore, there are considered to be Mandrakes and Womandrakes, the former being white, the latter black.

Mandrake has been described as a "drowsy syrup."

Issac Vossius, a seventeenth century scholar, states, It is

146

believed that in the mandrake lies the power of acquiring love.

The mandrake also has a soporific effect. In Shakespeare's *Antony and Cleopatra*, the queen exclaims,

> Give me to drink mandragora
> That I might sleep out this great gap of time
> My Antony is away.

For a like purpose it was administered by the ancient Greeks to surgical patients. In the Middle Ages, it was similarly recommended in the eleventh century by the philosopher and physician Avicenna.

In Persia, the mandrake was used to secure a husband's love.

Dioscorides, a Greek physician who served in the army of the Emperor Nero, calls mandrake Circaea, the plant of Circe, because its root was thought to be an efficacious love philtre.

He also refers to a wine concoction of mandrake root that was used in surgical operations. This concoction was also used in the preparation of philtres.

Many legends associated with the mandrake are incorporated in a novel entitled *Vampire*, by Hans Heinz-Ewers.

Mango

The following treatment is suggested in Hindu erotological literature as a stimulant.

Arris root, dressed with oil of mango. Placed for six months in a hole in the trunk of the sisu tree, then taken out, made into an ointment, and applied to the genitalia.

Manichaeans

A religious sect accused by St. Augustine of practising monstrous rites associated with erotic perversions,

... execrabilis superstitionis quadam necessitate cogantur electi eorum eucharisitiam cum semine humano sumere ut etiam inde sicut de aliis cibis quos accipiunt, substantia illa divina purgetur.

Marijuana

This drug, *cannabis sativa,* is a decided aphrodisiac.

Its use, however, involves grave dangers, both psychic and organic. There should be no contact with the drug without medical supervision.

Marjoram

An aromatic herb used in flavoring foods. Has some aphrodisiac virtue.

Marquis De Sade (1745-1814)

A French novelist and erotologist infamous for his own acts and for the scatological nature of his writings. These writings probe into obscure sexual psychology, perversions, numberless forms of sexuality. In regard to aphrodisiacs, de Sade includes food, flagellation, pills and ointments, mechanical apparatus. One of his most notorious works is *120 Journées de Sodome.* Other novels that are equally lascivious and perverted are *Juliette, Justine,* and *Le Petit Fils d'Hercule.*

From the Marquis de Sade is derived the term for the sexual perversion known as *sadism,* erotic satisfaction secured by the infliction of pain.

Marrow

Traditionally, bone marrow is a source of vitality. Hence a pâté of marrow was a common concoction for whetting amorous appetite.

The Roman poet Horace refers to dried marrow as a regular aphrodisiac.

Martial

An epigram by the Roman poet Martial on a perverted erotic practice runs as follows,

148

Paediconibus os olere dicis,
Hoc si, sicut ais, Fabulle, verum est,
Quid credis olere cunnilinguis?

Marzipan

A slice of marzipan followed by a drink of hippocras is an amatory prescription advised by Rabelais in his *Gargantua and Pantagruel*.

Masochism

A sexual perversion involving erotic pleasure through the infliction on oneself of pain or cruelty. Derived from the name of the Austrian novelist Leopold von Sacher-Masoch (1835-1895), who described the condition in his works.

Massage

Massage, particularly inguinal, was frequently resorted to by the ancients as an inducement to potency. Petronius, the Roman novelist, presents in the *Satyricon* a scene depicting such an operation.

The practice is frequently mentioned in Greek literature.

Mastic

An Arab aphrodisiac. A drink made from the fruit of the mastic-tree, pounded with honey and oil, was recommended for increasing sperm.

Mathematics

It has been at least an academic tradition, if no more, that mathematical studies militate against amatory inclinations.

Maypole

The maypole, the focal point of many traditional spring games and festivities, is believed to be a relic of ancient phallic worship.

Meaning of Phallus

The term phallus is reputedly of Phoenician origin.

In Sanskrit the root phal means *to burst forth,* to be fruitful. Phal itself also means a *ploughshare.*

In Biblical literature the root occurs in Genesis 46.9, And the sons of Reuben, Hannoch, and Phallu.

Phallu is believed to signify *the distinguished one, the one who divides;* a reference to sensual love.

Meat

Although Hindu religious customs proscribed the eating of meat, meat was believed to increase sexual power and .is often mentioned in this respect in Hindu sexological manuals. Lean, red meat in particular is credited with strong aphrodisiac effects.

Medea

An ancient witch who pervades Greek and Roman mythology. One of her specific faculties is the restoration of virility by means of magic charms. The Greek poet Euripides, in his tragic drama *Medea,* presents her giving encouragement to aged Aegeus,

Thus by the Gods shall thy desire of children be accomplished to thee, and thou thyself shalt die in happiness. But thou knowest not what this fortune is that thou hast found; but I will free thee from being childless, and I will cause thee to raise up offspring—Such charms I know.

Medieval Anecdote

Brasica eruca, sown in the garden of a monastery, was taken as a daily infusion by the monks, under the impression that it would cheer and rouse them from customary sluggishness. But the continued use of it produced such an aphrodisiac effect that the cenobites, as the chronicle relates, transgressed alike "their monastery walls and vows."

Medieval Charms

Bourchand, Bishop of Worms, in his *De Poenitentia Decretorum,* describes certain aphrodisiacal charms that were

150

practised by the women of his time. The text is of such a nature that it must be quoted in the original Latin,

Fecisti quod quaedam mulieres facere solent? Tollunt menstruum suum sanguinem et immiscunt cibo vel potui et dant viris suis ad manducandum vel ad bibendum ut plus diligantur ab eis.

Si fecisti, quinque annos per legitimas ferias poeniteas. Gustasti de semine viri tui ut propter tua diabolica facta plus in amorem exardesceret?

Si fecisti, septem annos per legitimas ferias poenitere debeas.

Fecisti quod quaedam mulieres facere solent?

Prosternunt se in faciem et discoopertis natibus iubent ut supra nudas nates conficiatur panis, ut eo decocto tradant maritis suis ad comedendum. Hoc ideo faciunt ut plus exardescant in amorem suum.

Si fecisti, duos annos per legitimas ferias poeniteas.

Fecisti quod quaedam mulieres facere solent? Tollunt piscem vivum et mittunt eum in puerperium suum, et tam diu ibi tenent, donec mortuus fuerit, et decocto pisce vel assato, maritis suis ad comedendum tradunt. Ideo faciunt ut plus in amorem suum exardescant.

Si fecisti, duos annos per legitimas ferias poeniteas.

Medieval Invocation

A medieval invocation directed toward amatory satisfaction is quoted by Voltaire in his *Lettres sur François Rabelais*. Voltaire's description is as follows,

Le secret consistoit à prendre un cheveu de la fille, on le plaçoit d'abord dans son haut-de-chausses; on faisoit une confession générale et on fesoit dire trois messes, pendant lesquelles on mettoit le cheveu autour de son col; on allumait un cièrge béni au dernier Evangile et on prononçait cette formule,

O Vierge! Je te conjure par la vertu du Dieu tout-

puissant, par les neuf choeurs des anges, par la vertu gos-
drienne, amène—moi icelle fille, en chair et en os, afin que
je la saboule à mon plaisir.

Medieval Remedy

A fourteenth century remedy for impotence that has been
contrived through magic spells is as follows,

Burdock seeds, pounded in a mortar. Add the left testis
of a three-year old goat, a pinch of powder from the back
hairs of a dog that is entirely white. The hairs to be cut on the
first day of the new moon and burned on the seventh day.
Infuse all these items in a bottle half filled with brandy.
Leave uncorked for 21 days, so that it may receive the astral
influence.

On the 21st day—that is, precisely the first of the following moon—cook the entire compound until a thick con-
sistency is reached. Then add four drops of crocodile semen,
and pass the mixture through a filter. Gather up the resultant
liquid and apply to the genitalia, and immediately the application will effect marvels.

Since crocodiles are rare in Europe, the semen of certain
dogs may be substituted. It is said that Cleopatra believed
in this substitution, since dogs were able to avoid extermina-
tion by the crocodiles on the banks of the Nile.

In any case, this experiment, says the tradition, has always
been successful, whether crocodiles or dogs are used.

Membrum

Among the Romans the genital organ of the hedgehog and
the wolf were among the ingredients used in aphrodisiac
concoctions.

Membrum Virile

In chapter 8 of *The Perfumed Garden*, Sheik Nefzawi
enumerates some fifty synonyms for the membrum virile.
Rabelais, in his *Gargantua et Pantagruel*, offers a similar

curious list. Modern French argot likewise is rich in erotic synonyms.

See *PERFUMED GARDEN*.

Menghus Faventinus

An early medical writer who says that nettles,

ont une propriété merveilleuse pour allonger, tendre, grossir et ériger le membre virile.

In this regard, a medieval poem, emphasizing the same subject, runs thus

> Une femme en mélancholie
> Pour faute d'occupation,
> Frottez moi le cul d'ortie.
> Elle aura au cul passion.

Rabelais, author of the famous and ribald *Gargantua et Pantagruel,* alluding to this mode of procuring the vigor necessary for amorous aggressiveness, says,

Se frotter le cul au panicaut, vrai moyen d'avoir au cul passion.

Panicaut was a species of thistle.

Mens Sana

The ancients realized that physical and psychical conditions are interrelated. Thus Juvenal, the Roman satirist, epitomized this view in his now proverbial phrase,

Mens sana in corpore sano.

A healthy mind in a healthy body.

Such a condition, however indirectly, is conducive to amatory proclivities.

Meretricious Synonyms

Dr. Jacobus X, author of *Untrodden Fields of Anthropology,* gives a list of synonyms for prostitute that covers some 200 descriptive terms. These names distinguish the women according to physical appearance, physiological manoeuvres, locale, remuneration, and temperament.

The Romans similarly had a large number of variants for such women.

See *JACOBUS*.

Mescaline

A substance derived from the tufts of a cactus called *Peyotl* or *Lophophora Williamsii* or *Anhalonium Lewinni*. The plant grows wild in Mexico and Texas.

This cactus appears as a cluster of small button-like growths or discs, the main root being underground. The small growths, when dried, are known as peyotl or mescal buttons. They are of bitter taste and of leathery texture. In Mexican folklore the use of this drug is well attested.

Peyotl was known to the Indians of South America, and was also used in Aztec religious rites.

The cactus was called "the flesh of gods," and was an object of worship among the Indian priests.

The Spaniards who invaded Mexico called the cactus "Devil Flesh."

In South America, the harvesting of mescal buttons is a religious ceremony. In some locations stone statues are fashioned in the shape of buttons and are an object of worship. A similar form of veneration is associated with mushrooms, which also produce a mescaline-like substance.

In the course of time, the use of peyotl extended through Mexico and Central and North America. Although the use of the plant was prohibited, the Indians continued in their traditional ways, taking the buttons in an infusion.

Peyotl eating, as a tribal habit, is current at the present time and retains its substitutional characteristic as a replacement of the Christian sacrament.

At the turn of last century, scientific investigations began to examine the properties of the cactus and its effects on the human body. An experiment by a physician disclosed the remarkable visions that resulted from swallowing several doses of mescal buttons. Havelock Ellis in 1902 and Aldous Huxley in 1954 and again in 1956 experienced the effects of the drug and described their own personal sensations. Huxley the novelist did so in two notable books, *The Doors of Perception* and *Heaven and Hell.*

Briefly, the characteristic symptoms that appear in peyotl intoxication are visual hallucinations and delusions, associated with "horror chambers." Sexual desires also increase. In any case, the drug is dangerous without proper medical or psychiatric supervision.

Middle Ages

In the Middle Ages, as a result of commercial traffic between the continent of Europe and the East, the Crusades and other wars, travelers' tales, knowledge of philtres, aphrodisiacs, and other sexual stimulants spread from the Arabs and the Moors, from Egypt and India into the European herbals, pharmacopeias, and apothecaries' lore, and, on a more indeterminate level, among alchemists, wizards, and occultists.

Philtres in particular were in great demand. Their ingredients were miscellaneous, sometimes repulsive, but all the more credited with effective results in promoting amatory practices and consummations.

Miletus

The ancient wealthy city of Miletus, an Ionian city in Asia Minor, was a centre for the manufacture of aphrodisiac apparatus called *olisboi* or *bauba* in Greek.

Milk

Among the Arabs, washing the genitals with asses' milk was considered a means of stimulating vigor. Poppaea, wife of the Roman Emperor Nero, is said to have bathed in asses' milk, for beautifying purposes.

155

Mimnernus

The seventh century B.C. poet of Colophon was the first Greek lyric poet who hymned the sexual pleasures of men and women.

Mineral Waters

Bathing in certain mineral waters has for centuries been an aphrodisiac device. The procedure was familiar to the ancient Romans, who constantly practiced it in resorts throughout the Roman Empire.

In Arabic manuals dedicated to erotic counsel, recommendations are given for such bathing to all who are intent on maintaining or increasing sexual vigor.

Radio-active baths are said to act favorably in a sexual direction. So too with arsenical springs, cold water treatment, and hydrotherapy.

Mint

Aromatic plant used in flavoring foods. Reputed to have aphrodisiac properties.

Mistress-Goddess

King Ptolemy II, who belongs in the third century B.C., built a temple, according to the Greek biographer Plutarch, dedicated to Belestiche, his mistress, and named his mistress Aphrodite Belestiche.

Mixed Drinks

Cognac, with the addition of a little paprika and the yolk of an egg, is considered an effective aphrodisiac aid.

Mixoscopy

Secret observation of the sexual act and, by extension, of erotic activities designed to stimulate the observer.

See *VOYEURISM*.

In Homer's *Odyssey*, Hephaestus, husband of the goddess Aphrodite, invited all the gods to observe the lascivious spectacle of his wife in sexual embrace with Ares, the war

156

god. But in this case observation does not involve secrecy.

Among the ancient Tyrrhenians also mixoscopy was prevalent.

The Greek historian Herodotus describes an instance of mixoscopy in the tale of King Candaules. The King, proud of his wife's beauty, coaxed his friend Gyges to conceal himself in the nuptial chamber and witness the undressing of the queen. The queen, aware of the situation, was shamed, and made this offer to Gyges, "Either slay Candaules and become my lord and gain the kingdom of Lydia, or be content to die at once yourself where you are." Gyges slew Candaules, married the queen, and became ruler of Lydia.

Moh

The Moh tree, botanically *Bassia Latifolia*, produces flowers rich in sugar, used in India in the manufacture of the liquor *arrack*.

The pith of the Moh tree pounded, mixed with cow's milk, is taken as a wholesome drink.

The *Ananga-Ranga*, the Hindu compendium of sexology, recommends this recipe for the restoration of virility.

Mohabbazin

Egyptian actors who made a practice of transvestism.

See *TRANSVESTISM*.

Mollusca

The mollusca, and testaceous animals in particular, have been considered to be of potency in an amatory sense.

Moly

A lengendary plant, with white flowers and black root, endowed with magic virtues. In Homer, Hermes gives the herb to Ulysses to protect him against the wiles of Circe. Usually identified with Allium Moly, wild garlic. John Milton, in *Paradise Lost*, mentions the plant, moly.

That Hermes once to wise Ulysses gave.

Also Tennyson in the *Lotus Eaters,* beds of amaranth and moly.

The plant was associated with sexual implications.

Although it is not definitively identifiable, moly may well be a Phoenician term, or an Egyptian one used in Greek in a generic sense. It has also been suggested that moly may be equated with *Peganum Harmala,* that is, wild rue, a plant indigenous to Southern Europe and Asia Minor.

Monks' Anti-Aphrodisiacs

For anti-aphrodisiac purposes monks used to make an emulsion of the seeds of agnus castus "steeped in Nenuphar water, and of which they daily drank a portion, wearing at the same time round their loins a girdle made of its branches."

Monks' Use of Camphor

In the seventeenth century monks were compelled to smell and masticate camphor for the purpose of extinguishing concupiscence.

Most Dangerous Drugs

Four of the most dangerous drugs are cocaine, opium, cannabis, and mescaline.

Drugs such as these are habit-forming, hallucinogenic, affecting the nervous system and the mind, producing cataclysmic organic deteriorations often resulting in agonizing death.

Most Popular Aphrodisiac

Among the ancient Greeks, onions are most frequently mentioned as a stimulus to sexual desire.

Mouse

A person smeared with the excrement of a mouse was rendered impotent, according to Pliny the Elder.

Mugwort

In the Orient, this plant was associated with amatory tendencies.

Mukhannathun

In Arab countries, men who practice transvestism.
See *TRANSVESTISM*.

Muller, Johannes

Author of a doctorial dissertation entitled *De Febre Amatoria*, published in 1689. He discusses in particular sexual conditions relating to women. Hellebore, he asserts, is a decided anti-aphrodisiac. As aphrodisiac aids, on the other hand, he recommends rich banquets that create a sense of euphoria and thus indirectly stimulate amatory inclinations. In regard to drinking, he recommends moderation. In this connection he quotes a short poem of a certain Henry Stephan,

> I pour out three goblets
> for wise men.
> One for health, that they will first drink.
> Then, one for love and pleasure.
> The third drink, for sleep.
> Those who drink the last goblet and
> have a reputation for sagacity will
> straightway return to their own homes.

Mushrooms

Arabs consider the eating of mushrooms as an aphrodisiac aid.

There are, however, many varieties of mushrooms that have toxic properties. Two thousand years ago these toxic properties were already common knowledge. In the Middle Ages, also, medical texts refer to these characteristics. Cases are also cited of dried mushrooms, mixed with food or wine, being administered to prospective victims. In the sixteenth century, an Italian Cardinal, living in Rome, had a preparation made of granules of dried Amanita muscaria and secreted in a ring that he wore on his finger. The poison was thus ready to hand whenever necessary.

Musical Stimulus

A man who wishes to subjugate a woman, according to an erotic manual long in use in India, should play on a reed pipe. The pipe is to be dressed with the juice of the bahupadika plant, the tabernamontana coronaria, the costus speciosus, the pinus deodora, the euphorbia antiquorum, the vajra and the kantaka plant.

Musk

A brown, bitter, volatile substance, extracted from a gland near the genitals of the musk-deer and of a species of goat indigenous to Tartary. In Persia and Tibet musk is used in food for its amatory properties.

The odor of musk, according to the Hindu *Kama Sutra,* is associated with the ideal woman.

One Arab writer comments on the efficacy of perfuming oneself with musk as an aid before sexual activity.

In Oriental stories musk often appears as an enticing erotic factor.

See *PERFUMES*.

Musk Internally

Taken internally, musk was formerly believed to produce aphrodisiac sensations.

An old medical record relates that by means of musk the genital power of a man in his eightieth year was resuscitated.

Mustard Baths

Hot mustard baths have been recommended as assisting the libido in the case of women.

Mustard Seed

A strong infusion of mustard seed was formerly believed to be an effective amatory stimulant.

Mustela Piscis

The brains of the mustela piscis were held in high esteem by women, as an aphrodisiac.

Mutton

Mutton, eaten with caraway seed, is eaten as an aphrodisiac among Arabs.

Mutunus

Also identified with Tutunus. An ancient Roman obscene sexual deity.

St. Augustine has this comment to make, equating the deity with Priapus,

In celebratione nuptiarum super Priapi scaphum nova nupta sedere iubebatur.

Lactantius, one of the Fathers of the Church, who flourished in the fourth century A.D., makes equally condemnatory remarks,

et Mutunus in cuius sinu pudendo nubentes praesident, ut illarum pudicitiam prius deus delibasse videatur.

Arnobius, another Church Father, of the fourth century A.D., similarly fulminates against the practice,

Etiamne Tutunus, cuius immanibus pudendis horrentique fascino vestras inequitare matronas et auspicabile ducitis et optatis?

Myropolia

In Roman times, shops where perfumes were concocted and sold. Such perfumes were generally intended as excitations for sexual purposes, and included ingredients imported from every corner of the Roman Empire, and even beyond, from Spain and India, from Egypt and the Northern frontiers.

161

These perfumeries were also used as places of assignation and sexual rendezvous.

Myrrh

A compound of eggs boiled with myrrh, pepper, and cinnamon, taken on several successive days, is recommended by Arabs for strengthening amorous vigor.

See *PERFUMES*.

This gum is especially prized in the Orient, used as a medicinal aid in various illnesses as well as an erotic stimulant.

Myrtle

In the Middle Ages pulverized myrtle leaves were applied to the body as a sexual stimulation.

A putative love tonic was made from the water in which myrtle leaves and flowers had been steeped. Used in many European countries. An old recipe advises,

The flowers and leaves of myrtle, two handfuls, infuse them in two quarts of spring water, and a quart of white wine, for twenty-four hours, and then distil them in a cold still and this will be of a strong scent and tincture, and by adding more or less of the myrtle you may make it stronger or weaker as you please. This beautifies, and mixed with cordial syrups is a good cordial and inclines those that drink it to be very amorous.

N

Nail Parings
Among the Romans, used in magic rites for aphrodisiac purposes.

Nakedness
To encourage sensual excitation, the Greeks had naked girls present at their feasting and drinking entertainments.
Similar practices are contemporary "stag parties."

Naples
In the Kingdom of Naples, in the town of Trani, during Carnival a wooden statue was carried in procession. It represented an entire gigantic Priapus, with prominent phallus. This member was called by the people Il Santo Membro, *The Holy Member.*

The ancient ceremony was evidently a relic of antiquity, a celebration in honor of Bacchus. It continued until the beginning of the eighteenth century, when it was finally abolished by ecclesiastical authority.

Natural Philosophy
Next to Mathematics, the study of natural philosophy tends to have anti-aphrodisiac effects. One erotologist adds, "requiring, as it does, the unremitting attention of the student, his perambulation of the open country, and the personal observation of all animated objects."

Necks of Snails
This recipe, taken with a little wine, was used by the Romans as an aphrodisiac.

Nedde

In Arab countries, a mixture of various perfumes, with benzoin and amber predominating, is so called. This mixture, which is black in color, is formed into a small cylinder and used aphrodisiacally.

Nefzawi

Umar ibn Muhammed al-Nefzawi, the author of *The Perfumed Garden,* lived in Southern Tunisia. Here he produced his remarkable erotic manual. The preface says that "the author was animated by the most praiseworthy intentions."

The Introduction itself warns that the work is not to be considered as a lascivious or obscene text, but highly motivated, for the Sheik begins: Praise be given to God, who has placed man's greatest pleasure in the genitalia of women and has destined the partes genitales of man to afford the greatest enjoyment to women.

The subjects of the manual range from sexual physiology to generation. A chapter is devoted to men who are held in contempt. Another treats of women who deserve to be praised. The deceits and treacheries of women, in erotic matters, are exposed. Medicines, aphrodisiacs, and sexual rites are discussed with great precision and lucidity.

Nepenthes

A drug or potion frequently mentioned by Homer, especially in the *Odyssey,* as having the effect of banishing sorrow or mental trouble. It has been variously identified, with opium, hashish, and particularly the *Panax Chironium* of Theophrastus, the third century B.C. Greek philosopher who wrote on plants.

Theophrastus asserts that, infused in wine, this drug was administered as an aphrodisiac.

A variant name for the drug is nepenthe.

To Homer himself the drug is "the gods' drink."

164

Newton

It is recorded that Sir Isaac Newton, the famous mathematician, is reputed to have lived without ever having had sexual intimacy.

See *MATHEMATICS*.

Nicotine

The nicotine in tobacco has been held to produce anaphrodisiac effects, in spite of such literary commendation as J. M. Barrie's *My Lady Nicotine*.

Ninjin

A root highly regarded by the Japanese. It has properties that putatively are analogous to the aphrodisiac virtues of the mandrake.

See *MANDRAKE*.

Nostrums

Many nostrums and traditional medicaments are mentioned throughout Greek literature as aphrodisiac stimulants. Papyri are also extant in which advice is given regarding ithyphallic competence. One such papyrus, rich in detail, is preserved in the Louvre, in Paris.

Nuoc-Man

An aphrodisiac sauce, consisting of extract of decayed fish, much in use in the Far East, especially among the Chinese. It contains the two basic aphrodisiac elements, phosphorus and salt.

The sauce is often spiced with pimento and garlic.

Nutmeg

An aromatic seed of a tree native to the East Indies. Used to spice food. Highly prized in the Orient as an aphrodisiac, especially among Chinese women.

Nutrition

Experiments have demonstrated that sexual interest and

sexual desire increase with nutritional satisfaction, and that inversely a lowering of nutritional diet coincides with a diminution of sex expression. As a general rule, therefore, any kind of faulty nutrition will affect sexual ability. The importance of proper diet is emphasized or implicit in all manuals of erotology, both European and Oriental. For continued virility, a balanced diet would consist of the consumption of adequate quantities of fats, minerals, carbohydrates, and proteins.

Sexual stimulants are indicated in Ben Jonson's *Volpone*.

recipts

To please the belly and the groin.

Nux Vomica
A drug that may have a stimulating aphrodisiac effect, but also causes hallucinations. Dangerous to use.

Nymphaea
A Hindu aphrodisiac, in the form of a compound applied to the body, is, oil of hogweed, echites putescens, the sarina plant, yellow amaranth, and the leaf of the nymphaea.

Nymphs
As symbols of the provocations of sexual enjoyment, in Greek mythology the nymphs roamed the streams and forests, in search of handsome youths to favor with their embraces, sometimes even the wild satyrs of the woods won their favors.

O

Obscene Literature

Such literature has always been considered a powerful though indirect amatory stimulus. A nineteenth century erotologist states, "though the descriptions are cloaked in the most elegant phraseology, obscene literature taints and corrupts the mind of the unsuspecting reader." He refers particularly to "novels, such as, under the pretext of describing the working of the human heart, draw the most seducing and inflammatory pictures of illicit love, and throw the veil of sentimental philosophy over the orgies of debauchery and licentiousness. Nothing is more perilous to youth, especially of the female sex, than this description of books."

Octopus

The sepia octopus was once in great repute as an aphrodisiac. In the Roman comedy writer, Plautus, a scene occurs in his *Casina* in which an old man has just been purchasing some at the fish market.

Ointment

Among the Arabs, an ointment, unidentified in composition, but called the Balm of Judea or of Mecca, was used as an aphrodisiac.

See *PERFUMES*.

Old Recipe

An old European recipe, that was reputed to have been a potent aphrodisiac, consisted of cooked onions in a salad, mixed with oil, pepper, salt, and vinegar.

Olibanum

An aromatic resin once used in medicine. Now used as an

incense. It was known to the Greeks and the Romans. The Arabs compound it with honey and nutmeg as a sexual specific.

Olibanum is the Biblical frankincense. In the East, and in the Middle Ages, it was prized for its perfume. Among the Turks, an exciting compound consists of olibanum, myrrh, camphor, musk, in pulverized form. The resultant perfume is said to affect the genitals.

See *FRANKINCENSE*.

Ololuigui

This compound is related to mescaline and is obtained from a tropical plant called *rivea corynbosa*.

See *MESCALINE*.

This drug produces, along with visual hallucinations, sexual excitements. Highly dangerous.

Onions

Onions and similar bulbous plants have a legendary reputation for aphrodisiac qualities. The Roman poet Ovid, in his *Remedy for Love,* recommends the onion. Martial, the Roman epigrammatist, advises, If your wife is old and your member is exhausted, eat onions in plenty. Another, later, poet, Columella declares that onions inflame and animate girls.

In the case of men, onions add virility, in women, they purify the blood.

Oriental dishes intended as aphrodisiacs frequently contain onions. A popular dish among Arabs is a compound of onions and egg yolks.

Onion Seed

In *The Perfumed Garden,* Nefzawi suggests this stimulant,

Pound onion seed, sift it, mix it with honey. Stir the mixture well. Take this concoction while still fasting.

See *PERFUMED GARDEN*.

Another Arab dish recommended for sexual potency is

onions boiled with condiments and aromatic spices, then fried in oil and yolk of eggs. The preparation is to be taken on several successive days.

A Greek comedy writer says,

Onions are hard to digest, though nourishing and strengthening to the stomach; they are cleansing but they weaken the eyesight, and they also stimulate sexual desire.

According to the Greek physician Galen, pounded onion seed, mixed with honey and taken while undergoing fasting, has aphrodisiac qualities.

Opium

This extract from the poppy was known to the ancient Greeks. It is described by Dioscorides, who flourished in the first century A.D. In the Middle Ages it was used for medicinal purposes, also for eating and smoking. Later, it acquired a putative aphrodisiac significance.

Opium is largely used by the Chinese as a sexual provocation, both by men and women; but it is attended by such dangerous effects as to warrant total avoidance of the drug.

See *DRUGS*.

Dr. Venette declares that opium is an aphrodisiac, but he utters a grave warning on its use.

He declared that he experimented with the drug himself.

Used among Turkish soldiers, by whom it is known as *amsiam*.

See *VENETTE*.

Thomas De Quincey, the English essayist, was an opium addict for some twenty-five years. In his *Confessions of an English Opium-Eater* he describes how he was first introduced to the drug as a remedy for toothache.

The Hindu name for opium is chandu, it is both eaten and smoked, and is said to increase vitality.

The poppy, from which the opium is extracted, was cultivated as a garden flower eight centuries B.C.

It is mentioned by the Greek poet Homer in his *Iliad*,
> Down sank his head, as in a garden sinks
> A ripened poppy charg'd with vernal rains;
> So sank his head beneath his helmet's weight.

Hippocrates, the Greek physician who belongs in the fifth century B.C., knew of poppy juice.

Vergil, the Roman epic poet, refers to it thus, Sleep-giving poppy

and,

Poppy pervaded with Lethean sleep.

Cornelius Nepos, a Roman biographer of the first century B.C., alludes to the plant.

In the first century A.D. opium was known as a medicine, and is mentioned in this respect by the Roman encyclopedist Pliny the Elder.

As a stimulant, the use of opium became widely diffused from the seventh century on, in Arab countries.

The Portuguese sailors and explorers of the Middle Ages were also familiar with the drug.

Vespucci, the traveler and geographer, mentions opium as part of a cargo that was brought from India to Lisbon in 1501.

The Dutch traveler Linschoten, in his account of his voyages in 1596 entitled *Discourse of Voyages unto Ye Easte and West Indies,* says,

"They (i.e., the Indians) use it most for lecherie . . . although such as eate much thereof are in time altogether unable to company with a woman and whollie dried up, for it drieth and whollie cooleth man's nature that use it."

A commentary on the need for moderation in eating, drinking, and the taking of specifically recommended herbs, ointments, and so on.

Opium is *papaver somniferum* in Latin, that is sleep-producing poppy.

In ancient Sumeria, opium was known as the "plant of joy." It was known in the Age of the Pharaohs and throughout Biblical times. King David, subject to fits of depression, was cured of his condition by means of a potion, of which the chief ingredient was opium.

In Old Egypt the seeds of the white poppy were mixed with flour and honey and made into a cake.

The imperial physicians at the court of the Emperor Nero used potions compounded with opium. Theophrastus refers to opium medicinally.

From Asia Minor, about the fifteenth century, the poppy was introduced into India. In Macedonia and Persia it began to be cultivated in the eighteenth century.

English medicine received its first experiments with opium in the Middle Ages from Venice via Germany.

Laudanum, a derivative of opium, was the name given to a secret remedy concocted by the occultist Paracelsus, in the sixteenth century. The legend runs that he carried opium in the hilt of his sword.

Morphine is another derivative of opium. Opium and its derivatives are all habit-forming drugs, dangerous to take, and fatal in their effects.

Opium is a dangerous habit-forming drug. It removes inhibitions and replaces them by emotional excitements. The sense of moral responsibility is lost, together with will power, a common effect of some drugs.

The aphrodisiac effect is due to the creation of this excitement and the abandonment of restraints and also to the resultant erotic dreams created by the habit.

Sexual consummation, however, is usually inhibited.

Opium and Mandrake
Queen Bernice, wife of Ptolemy, fourth century B.C., received a sedative before the birth of her child, that was reputedly a mixture of opium and mandrake.

See *OPIUM* and *MANDRAKE*.

Opotherapy
Treatment by means of juices or extracts. Sexual ex-

171

citation has been aroused or restored in some cases by the administration of genital gland extracts from animals.

Such extracts contain hormones conducive in particular cases to amatory activity. But such a procedure must not be adopted without authoritative medical control.

Oracular Aphrodisiac
In an ancient Greek comedy an elderly character consults an oracle for aid in his senescent condition. The counsel involved a dish of lentils.

Orchid
Etymologically, this name signifies in Greek *testes*. This plant, whose shape has more than symbolic similarity to the male genitalia, has had an unwarranted reputation as an aphrodisiac.

Orchis Hircina
The root of this plant, in ancient times, formed the basis of a powerful aphrodisiac called satyrion.

See *SATYRION*.

Orchis Morio
A plant of the satyrion species, used in Turkey as a stimulant. It grows on the mountains near Istanbul.

See *SATYRION*.

Organotherapy
In sexual disorders, the treatment consists, in one direction, of the consumption of the genitalia of animals—stags, roosters, asses—as a means of recovering sexual potency. The testes of animals were also used for this purpose, and meals were compounded largely with these ingredients. The practice was commonly in use among the Romans, in the Orient, notably in India, and during the Middle Ages. It was recommended and used as late as the beginning of the nineteenth century.

Brillat-Savarin, the famous French gourmet, mentions such dishes.

Oriental Recipe

A medieval physician, Zacutus Lusitanus, in his *Praxis Medica Admiranda*, describes such a recipe as being composed of, bole Tuccinum, musk, ambergris, aloes-wood, red and yellow sanders (pterocarpus santalinus), mastic, sweet-flag (calamus aromaticus), galanga, cinnamon, rhubarb, Indian myrobalon, absinthe, pounded on precious stones.

An old encyclopedia comments on this prescription,

It imparts a sweetness to the breath, is a valuable medicine in all nervous complaints, and is esteemed as a prolonger of life and an exciter of venery.

Origanum Majorana

Marjoram. An aromatic herb used in cookery.

Among the ancients, especially the Romans, marjoram was known to have an aphrodisiac value.

Origen

One of the principal Fathers of the Church, who flourished in the third century A.D. In order to eliminate all carnal tendencies, he operated as follows,

Ut corpus ab omni venerea labe mundum servaret, omnique suspicione careret, sectis genitalibus membris, eunuchum se fecit.

Orion

The sexual proclivities of Orion, who was fabled by the Greeks to be a giant, or a great hunter, were so violent that he ravished the daughter of his guest Oenopion, King of Chios. He also attacked Artemis, who sent a scorpion to sting him to death. Myths such as these symbolize the powerful amatory urges of the ancient Greeks.

Orthaon

The name of one of the twelve mythological creatures

known as Centaurs. A centaur was part human, part equine, and was associated with a cult on Mount Helicon. Orthaon itself means ithyphallic.

Osphresiology

The study of aromas and olfactory reactions. In a special anthropological sense, the study concerns aromas and sexual relationships.

Repulsive odors of functional performances, body emanations, especially from the area of the genitalia, may produce intense erotic susceptibilities.

Other aromas, vegetable scents, and animal odors, have been enlisted for amatory stimulus, reacting, with profound sexual repercussions, on the olfactory nerves.

Mutual smelling, in fact, is an aphrodisiac procedure itself.

In the Orient, and among certain tribes such as the Chittagongs, lovers, instead of kissing in the occidental fashion, inhale each other's odor by nasal contacts.

In an anti-aphrodisiac sense, on the other hand, unpleasant odors arising from food mastication, decayed teeth, tobacco breath often create erotic repulsion. In extreme perverted cases, again, such odors may have an amatory appeal.

Ovid

In his *Ars Amatoria*, the Roman poet Ovid describes a number of items that were, in his time, associated, sometimes wrongly, with aphrodisiac properties,

Some teach that herbs will efficacious prove,
But in my judgment such things poison love.
Pepper with biting nettle-seed they bruise,
With yellow pellitory wine infuse.
Venus with such as this no love compels,
Who on the shady hill of Eryx dwells.
Eat the white shallots sent from Megara

Or garden herbs that aphrodisiac are,
Or eggs, or honey on Hymettus flowing,
Or nuts upon the sharp-leaved pine-trees growing.

Ovid on Aphrodisiacs

The Roman poet Ovid (43 B.C.—c. 17 A.D.) condemns, in his *Ars Amatoria* aphrodisiac aids such as hippomanes, magic herbs, exorcism formulas, love philtres. They have no effect, he declares. For even the enchantresses Circe and Medea could not, by their black arts, prevent the unfaithfulness of Odysseus and Jason.

Ovid on Philtres

The Roman poet Ovid, who wrote a poetic erotic guide called *Ars Amatoria,* The Art of Love, asserts that philtres are futile in the contest of love,

Pallid philtres given to girls were of no avail. Philtres harm the mind and produce an impact of madness.

See *PHILTRES.*

Oysters

In spite of the intriguing short story by Emile Zola, the oyster does not seem to deserve its reputation as an aphrodisiac. For its succulence and food value, however, reference may be made to the Roman poet Ausonius. He has a poem of fifty-one lines, exclusively dedicated to oysters and their beds, from Bordeaux to Marseilles and from the Hellespont to Caledonia.

In all probability, the association of oysters with sexual activity stems from the fact that, on the half shell, the oyster has similarities with the *pudenda muliebria.*

The Roman satirist, Juvenal, on the other hand, attributes aphrodisiac qualities to oysters,

For what cares the drunken dame
(take head or tail), to her 'tis much the same
Who at deep midnight on fat oysters sup.

175

An early scholar, commenting on Juvenal, adds,
  In marvelous fashion oysters are a
  stimulant, hence shameless and
  lascivious women ate oysters in order
  to be more apt for the amatory act.

P

Padmini

The Lotus-Woman. In Hindu erotic literature, the ideal woman. Gifted physically and emotionally with all the perfect characteristics of Oriental feminine seductiveness.

Palatine Anthology

A collection of fifteen books of Greek poems, many of them describing erotic scenes, amatory and sensual incidents, and occasionally offering love advice that is realistic and at times cynical.

Pamphila

A Roman matron of the first century A.D., who wrote a little monograph, no longer extant, entitled *On Sexual Enjoyments*.

Pan

A Greek god of the mountains and forests whose most dominant characteristic is continuous lustfulness. His goat feet are associated with the goat itself, whose characteristic is a vast amorous propensity.

The attendants of Pan are satyrs, equally characterized by lustful inclinations. The Greek expression pan signifies *everything,* and the implication is that the entire cosmos is permeated and conditioned by the procreative force.

Pander

According to the Greek biographer Plutarch, a certain Spartan Polyagnus acted as a pander for his own wife. It was not a condemnatory practice, as in Sparta the essential factor in marriage was eugenic propagation.

Another Greek, Stephanus, was a pimp for both his own wife and his daughter.

Pannychis

A Greek festival in honor of Aphrodite, goddess of love. At this festival the hetairae, the amatory companions of men, roamed the dark streets during the night and sold their favors readily and indiscriminately for a small fee.

Pantomime

In Greek and Roman pantomimic performances the erotic theme was dominant. The subjects so treated dealt with the amatory exercises of the divinities, incest, homosexuality, and even, as the Greek satirist Lucian and the Roman epigrammatist Martial mention, love scenes between human beings and animals, for example, the passion of Queen Pasiphaë for a bull, and the Thessalonian woman enamoured of an ass.

All such performances had their erotic reactions on the public spectators.

Paprika

Hungarian red pepper. This condiment is credited with decided erotic impulses.

Paracelsus

A sixteenth century occultist who wrote about love philtres.

Parkinson, John

A seventeenth century writer, author of *Theatrum Botanicum,* published in 1640, who describes the uses of the Chinese narcotic called *Ma Fu Shuan.*

Partes Genitales

These organs, in the case of the rooster, serve as a powerful aphrodisiac, according to Mery, in his *Traité Universel des Drogues Simples.*

178

Parthenius

Parthenius of Nicaea belongs in the first century B.C. Author of a collection of stories of unhappy love, a kind of amatory reference book.

Pastry

Honey, ginger, syrup of vinegar, pellitory, cardamoms, cinnamon, garlic, long pepper, nutmeg, hellebore, and Chinese cinnamon, compounded into a cake are a specific Arab prescription for potency.

In the Middle Ages in particular aphrodisiacs were commonly kneaded into breads and pastries intended for particular persons or used in intimate banquets.

Paulus Silentiarius

A court official of the Emperor Justinian, sixth century A.D. Author of a number of epigrams of an arousing erotic nature.

Pauravisia

In Melanesian mythology, a phallic snake.

Peaches

Considered to have stimulating aphrodisiac value.

Peas

A dish that, according to Nefzawi, the author of *The Perfumed Garden*, creates passion, is prepared as follows,

Green peas boiled with onions, powdered with cinnamon, ginger, and cardamoms well pounded.

See *PERFUMED GARDEN*.

Pepper

Used as a condiment. Compounded with nettle-seed, the preparation was credited with exciting sexual impulses. Both white and red pepper are considered to have this property.

179

Perch

In the head of this fish there are small stones that sorceresses used in concocting love-philtres.

Perfumed Beds

Perfume as an amatory enticement is mentioned in the Bible, in connection with the adulterous woman,

I have perfumed my bed with myrrh, aloes, and cinnamon.

Come, let us take our fill of love until the morning; let us solace ourselves with loves.

Proverbs: 7. 17-18.

Perfumed Garden

A manual of Arabian erotic techniques, written in the sixteenth century by Sheikh al-Imam Abu Abd-Allah al-Nefzawi. Translated into French in the nineteenth century, also into English by the Orientalist Sir Richard Burton.

Perfumed Genitalia

From the earliest times in Egypt, in Hellenistic Alexandria, in eighteenth century France, and in some parts of Europe and the Orient to this day, women have had a practice of using perfumed pads. The intention was to arouse the utmost sensory excitation in their lovers. The perfumed sacs were used in the *pudenda muliebria*.

Perfumes

Among the Romans in particular, erotic impulses were encouraged by the lavish use of exotic perfumes and unguents. Perfumes were used on the body, on the head and hair, and on garments. Civet and ambergris were especially popular among the wealthy, leisurely, sophisticated set. Aromatic spices, too, were an aid to sweetened breath. *Foliatum* was an ointment prepared from spikenard. Another perfume was known as *nicerotiana,* named after its originator Nicerotas. Myrrh, cinnamon, sweet marjoram, and the plum-like myrobalan fruit were likewise usual ingredients of aromatic preparations.

That strange synthesis of East and West, Lafcadio Hearn, made a brief study of perfumes in relation to women.

Arab erotic manuals stress the importance of perfumes, for both men and women, as an indirect and subtle stimulant in amorous techniques.

The significance of aromas in sexology is also richly illustrated in the tales of the *Arabian Nights* and in *The Song of Songs.*

> his lips like lilies, dropping sweet smelling myrrh . . .
> thy name is an ointment . . .
> a bundle of myrrh is my well-loved unto me . . .
> hands dropped with myrrh, and my fingers with sweet smelling myrrh . . .
> ointment and perfumes rejoice the heart . . .
> aloes with all the chief perfumes . . .
> perfumes and sweet spices . . .
> beds of aromatic spices . . .

Ruth anointed herself with fragrant oils. Esther purified herself with oil of myrrh and sweet odors. Judith anointed herself with precious ointment.

Mohammed mentions his love of women and perfumes. Biographers write of men who gave out an enticing personal fragrance from their bodies. Plutarch, for instance, the Greek biographer, says that the body of Alexander the Great gave off a scent of violets. Goethe calls such men "human flowers."

Among primitive races and Orientals the olfactory kiss is believed to produce a powerful sexual reaction.

The novels of Emile Zola, especially *La Terre* and *Germinal,* and *A Rebours* and *Là-Bas,* by J.K. Huysmans, contain numerous allusions to the sexual impact made by both natural and concocted odors.

Aristophanes, the Greek comedy writer, also mentions perfumes in a sexual context in his play *Lysistrata.*

The Roman poet Horace refers to a lecherous old fop "scented with nard."

In his play *Volpone*, Ben Jonson has Volpone make this amatory offer to Celia,

Thy baths shall be the juice of July-flowers,
Spirit of roses, and of violets,
The milk of unicorns, and panthers' breath
Gathered in bags, and mixed with Cretan wines.
Our drink shall be prepared gold and amber;
Which we will take, until my roof whirl round
With the vertigo.

July-flowers, that is, Gillyflowers.

See *GILLYFLOWER*.

Persian Recipe

Cloves, cinnamon, and cardamoms. Put them in a jar and over them read backward a chapter of the Koran. Then fill the jar with rose water, and steep husband's shirt in it with a piece of parchment inscribed with his name and the names of four angels. Heat together over a fire. When the mixture boils, the husband's love will increase.

Perspiration

Often has a powerful amorous impact on the male. Henry III of Navarre and Henry IV are said to have inadvertently inspired a passion in Maria of Cleves and Gabrielle respectively through the transmission of a handkerchief used to wipe away perspiration.

Persuasive Method

Amatory intimacy, as all the erotic manuals warn, Hindu, Chinese, Arab, and Roman, should be preceded by enticing amorous preludes. Ovid, the Roman poet, suggests in his *Ars Amatoria* just such introductory tactile preludes to erotic consummation. He hints that Venus must not be unduly hurried,

182

Crede mihi, non est Veneris properanda voluptas, Sed
sensim tarda prolicienda mora.

Believe me, the pleasures of love must not be hastened,
but should be allured forth gently with lingering delay.

Perversities

Like the Romans, who had their pathici, ephebi, gemelli,
catamiti, amasii, the Chinese had similar perverts, whom they
designated by a variety of names,

sio kia a,

sio kia isia,

tshat sia kia,

ka thanga.

Perverts

Dr. Jacobus X, in his *Untrodden Fields of Anthropology*,
gives a list, covering three large pages, of synonyms for perverts. The locale, in most cases, is the Orient.

See *JACOBUS*.

Pesoluta

A plant called by the Roman encyclopedist Pliny the
Elder *pesoluta* was said to cause impotence.

Petit Souper

A Little Supper. A French custom, popular in the eighteenth century, that, by its intimacy and the offering of
specially prepared heartening dishes, was a decided factor
in increasing erotic sensibility among the few, selected guests.
Such instances of the marriage of love and gastronomy were
frequent in the more elegant houses of pleasure.

The Duc de Richelieu often had, as guests to these sup-
pers, his friends and their mistresses, all appearing *in puris
naturalibus*.

Petrarch

Fourteenth century Italian poet and humanist. Of love

he says that it is a hidden fire, a pleasing wound, a palatable poison, a bitter sweetness, a delightful sickness, a joyous torture, an indulgent death.

Pets Parfumés
In the sixteenth century, French professional beauties, in order to retain or acquire the love of some courtier or other, used tiny vesicles filled with musk. Bursting these vesicles at appropriate moments, the women enveloped their lovers in a provocative, sexually arousing atmosphere.

See *MUSK*.

Phallic Symbols
Such symbols, dedicated to the cosmic procreative force, appeared in the temple at Heliopolis in Syria, and in the shrines in Thebes, Egypt. The Temple at Karnak, also, was adorned with phallic reliefs.

Biblical mention occurs in Ezekiel 23.14,15,

. . . and that she increased her whoredoms; for when she saw men portrayed upon the wall, the images of the Chaldeans portrayed with vermilion,

Girded with girdles upon their loins, exceeding in dyed allure upon their heads, all of them princes to look at, after the manner of the Babylonians of Chaldea, the land of their nativity.

Phanes
Phanes Protogonos, that is, Phanes the First Born, was an ancient Greek bisexual ithyphallic divinity similar in many characteristics to Priapus.

See *PRIAPUS*.

Phanias
Phanias of Lesbos, an ancient Greek writer, who produced a political work, no longer extant, that was packed with erotic stories.

184

Pharmacopoeia

In old pharmacopoeias many formulas were enumerated, in which amber constituted the base.

These recipes were all directed toward amatory capacity, as their names imply, e.g.

Tablets of Magnanimity,

Electuary Satyrion,

Joy Powder.

Pheasant

Highly aphrodisiac in effect.

Most game is traditionally associated with amatory effects.

Philodemus

Philodemus of Gadara was a Greek Epicurean philosopher of the first century B.C. Author of a collection of erotic poems that range over the entire field of sexual exercises and variations, including orgiastic and drunken revels, adulteries, and every type of lewdness.

Philostratus

An ancient Greek writer, author of *The Life of Apollonius of Tyana,* packed with erotic stories, sexual perversions, and unique informative pieces on all kinds of amatory situations.

Phlyax

An ancient farcical performance, with ithyphallic actors, obscene and suggestive. The phlyax was popular in Southern Italy. It was accompanied by music and indecent dances and transvestism—all intended to arouse sexual feelings in the audience.

Philtre

A magic potion usually intended to induce amorous effects on the drinker. The ancient Greeks and Romans were familiar with the aphrodisiac purposes of such drinks. In his

Marriage Precepts, for instance, the historian Plutarch mentions them specifically. Exotic or repulsive ingredients generally formed the base of the potions and included briony, mandrake root, tobacco, the bones of frogs, betel nuts, sparrow liver, the genitals, entrails, testes of hare, hare kidney, fingers, human and animal excrement, blood and brains of sparrow, semen of stag, animal secretions, as well as flesh, brain, urine, ambergris, hoopee brains powdered into a cake, roast heart of humming bird, powdered. Shakespeare's *Macbeth* contains a scene depicting three witches concocting a potion.

The Spanish artist Goya, too, painted a witch in the act of preparing a philtre.

Love philtres have continuously been a folk means of inspiring passions. Many European legends and sagas of various types, together with ballads and popular beliefs, emphasize the erotic powers of such potions. The administration of such philtres still prevails in outlying areas, in secluded valleys, and agricultural districts, throughout the European continent.

The Romans dwell frequently and with descriptive detail on philtres. Horace speaks of potions to excite desire as if it were a matter of common knowledge. The poet Propertius refers to a philtre containing snake bones, a toad, and the feathers of a screech-owl. Apuleius the novelist, in the *Metamorphoses,* includes among such ingredients a skull torn from between the teeth of a wild beast.

In both civilized society as well as primitive communities copraphagous aphrodisiacs were in common use, urine, faeces of human beings and animals, fluids, intestinal organs. Pliny the Elder, the encyclopedist, the medieval occultist Paracelsus, the demonographer Reginald Scott, and J. C. Frommann, author of *De Fascinatione,* 1674, all mention such scatological items.

Among the Navajos cow ordure was similarly in demand. The Apaches treated human excrement as an erotic aid. In

Africa the Hottentots used urine to induce sexual stimulus.

Horace describes a typical love philtre, composed by the witch Canidia,

> Canidia crown'd with wreathing snakes
> Dishevell'd, thus the silence breaks,
> "Now the magic fire prepare,
> And from graves, uprooted tear
> Trees, whose horrors gloomy spread
> Round the mansions of the dead,
> Bring the eggs and plumage foul
> Of a midnight shrieking owl,
> Be they well besmear'd with blood
> Of the blackest venom'd toad,
> Bring the choicest drugs of Spain,
> Produce of the poisonous plain,
> Then into the charm be thrown,
> Snatch'd from famish'd bitch, a bone,
> Burn them all with magic flame,
> Kindled first by Colchian dame."

20

John Gay (1685-1732), in his play *The Shepherd's Week*, likewise assumes the contemporary effective usage of a love philtre,

> Straight to the 'pothecary's shop I went,
> And in love powder all my money spent;
> Behap what will, next Sunday after prayers,
> When to the ale house Lupperkin repairs,
> These golden flies into his mug I'll throw,
> And soon the swain with fervent love shall glow.

Shakespeare alludes to the practice of administering love charms in *Othello,*

> thou hast practis'd on her with foul charms,
> Abus'd her delicate youth with drugs or minerals
> That weaken motion.

187

So again in *A Midsummer Night's Dream,*
This man hath bewitch'd the bosom of my child,
Thou, thou, Lysander, thou hast given her rimes,
And interchang'd love-tokens with my child;
Thou hast by moonlight at her window sung,
With feigning voice, verses of feigning love;
And stol'n the impression of her fantasy
With bracelets of thy hair, rings, gawds, conceits,
Knacks, trifles, nosegays, sweetmeats, messengers
Of strong prevailment in unharden'd youth.

In *A Midsummer Night's Dream,* also, there is an allusion
to the pansy as an ingredient in the love philtre,
Oberon, That very time I saw, but thou couldst not,
Flying between the cold moon and the earth,
Cupid all arm'd, a certain aim he took
At a fair vestal throned by the west,
And loos'd his love-shaft smartly from his bow,
As it should pierce a hundred thousand hearts;
But I might see young Cupid's fiery shaft
Quench'd in the chaste beams of the wat'ry moon,
And the imperial votaress passed on,
In maiden meditation, fancy-free.
Yet mark'd I where the bolt of Cupid fell,
It fell upon a little western flower,
Before milk-white, now purple with love's wound,
And maidens call it Love-in-Idleness.
Fetch me that flower; the herb I show'd thee once,
The juice of it on sleeping eyelids laid
Will make or man or woman madly dote
Upon the next live creature that it sees.
Fetch me this herb; and be thou here again
Ere the leviathan can swim a league.
Puck, I'll put a girdle round about the earth
In forty minutes.

Oberon, Having once this juice,
I'll watch Titania when she is asleep,
And drop the liquor of it in her eyes,
The next thing then she waking looks upon,
Be it on lion, bear, or wolf, or bull,
On meddling monkey, or on busy ape,
She shall pursue it with the soul of love,
And ere I take this charm off from her sight,
As I can take it with another herb,
I'll make her render up her page to me.

In seventeenth century Scotland, an old chronicle relates that a necromancer was found who prepared certain philtres or poisons and enchanted tokens of love, especially a jewel of gold, set with divers precious diamond, or rubies . . . that had the secret and devilish force of alluring and forcing the person sought to expose her body, fame, and credit to the will and unlawful pleasure of the giver thereof.

A Scottish witch, Katherine Craigie, who flourished in the seventeenth century, promised a love-lorn widow, I will give you a grass, which being used at my direction, it will cause him to have no other woman but you.

Love philtres are prevalent in Irish legend and literature. One particularly macabre item is the "dead strip." A girl goes to a graveyard at night, exhumes a corpse that has been buried for nine days, and tears a strip of skin from it. This strip is tied round the leg or arm of her lover while he is asleep, and removed before he wakes. This procedure ensures the constancy of love.

In the Middle Ages, when witchcraft and thaumaturgic practices were rampant over Europe, sorceresses did a roaring trade in magic brews designed to excite passion or to preserve affection. These witches became primary and valuable consultants in these amatory challenges. The witch would suggest, to the love-sick knight, a procedure that involved fetishism. Hair from the loved woman, nail parings, some intimate garment impregnated with the wearer's perspiration or perfume had somehow to be secured. To the accompaniment of incantations, the witch would burn the gathered objects, reducing them to ashes. The ashes would be thrown into a drink, a goblet of wine, a glass of mead, to be drunk by the desired woman. And the passionate suppliant would be assured by the witch of the aphrodisiac effect of her ritual.

It happened that some philtres were effective, but a great many, concocted not only of repellent but poisonous ingredients, herbs, and drugs, led to disastrous results. Yet the demand for any means to attain sexual mastery was so intense, so continuous, so widespread, among princelings and peasants, serf and squire, kings and burghers, that peripatetic vendors, proclaiming with effrontery and assurance the efficacy of secret potions in their possession and oral recipes, reaped rich harvests throughout the European countries. The concoctions contrived by Italians were particularly in clamant demand, while the occult sciences of astrology and alchemy lent their support, by indirection or not, to the penetration of the aphrodisiac elements secreted in Nature.

Martin Delrio, a sixteenth century Spanish prosecutor of witchcraft and also a demonographer, in his Latin *Disquisitionum Magicarum Libri Sex,* Book I, Part I, Question III, discusses philtres and aphrodisiac stimulants, giving instances of their use known to him. He condemns all such practices as heretical and malefic, and associates them with witches and Satanic agencies.

Philtres in Rome

The use of potions, especially containing mandrake, is well attested for Roman Imperial times. The Emperor Julian, called the Apostate, writes as follows to his friend Callixenes,

But you, Callixenes, observe that Penelope's love for her

190

husband was always thus manifested. To this I answer, who but he that has habitually drunk mandragora can prefer in a woman conjugal affection to piety?

See *MANDRAKE*.

Phosphorus

Foods containing this element are considered of aphrodisiac significance.

Phosphorus has long been considered a powerful stimulant. It acts upon the generative organism, it is recorded, in a manner to cause the most violent priapisms.

Phylarchus

Ancient Greek historian. Wrote a voluminous history containing numerous amatory tales, also descriptions of remedies, roots, and other aphrodisiac treatments. Fragments of Phylarchus have survived in the encyclopedic work of Athenaeus.

See *ATHENAEUS*.

Pimento

Now used as a spice. In 1132, however, Peter the Venerable forbade the monks of Cluny to use it on account of its aphrodisiac effects.

When pimento and pepper are boiled together with a species of mallow, the resultant compound is applied to rice-flour poultices, which in turn are placed in contact with the lingam. This is a Chinese prescription that is highly hazardous but is used externally as a stimulant.

Pimpinella Anisum

The botanical name of anise, indigenous to the Levant. It was known to Dioscorides, the ancient Greek botanist. Both in European and in Arab countries, during the Middle Ages, anise has had a wide amatory reputation.

Pineapple

Often used formerly as an aphrodisiac.

Pine Seeds

In the Orient, greatly prized as an effective aphrodisiac.

Pistachio

Pistacia vera. A nut that is frequently mentioned in Arab erotic manuals for its aphrodisiac value.

Pisteriona

Also called *Hierobota*. Albertus Magnus, *De Secretis Mulierum,* states that this herb increases desire. The virtue of the plant is so potent that its mere possession is a stimulant.

Plaice

A fish of reputed aphrodisiac value.

Most fish have traditionally aphrodisiac properties.

Platina

Author of De Valetudine Tuenda, *On Preserving Health.* An early authority who praises, as an aphrodisiac, the flesh of partridge.

The flesh of the partridge, which is of good and easy digestion, is highly nutritious; it strengthens the brain, facilitates conception, and arouses the half-extinct desire for venereal pleasures.

Plautus

A Roman comedy writer of the second century B.C., whose plays, most of them still extant, are full of lively gusto, an atmosphere of bawdiness, riotous obscenities, and sexual emphasis that, in all, reflect the ordinary common level of Roman living and Roman ways and attitudes. In two of his plays, the *Mercator* and *Cistellaria,* he describes the emotional and contradictory reactions associated with being in love.

In the Middle Ages, many poets, among them Matthew of Vendôme, have similar things to say about their provocative sweethearts.

Ploss

Author of *Das Weib in der Natur und Völkerkunde.* Leipzig, 1895.

This medical authority discusses, with instances, the relation between the olfactory and the sexual senses.

See *PERFUMES.*

Plovers' Eggs

Stuffed with various spices, this dish, called Plovers' Eggs à la Du Barry, has the reputation of being irresistible to amorous assaults.

See *EGG.*

Plutarch

Greek philosopher and biographer of the first century A.D. In his *De Sanitate Tuenda Praecepta*—Precepts for the Preservation of Health—he discusses dietetics. He also alludes to the arousing effect of satyrion.

See *SATYRION.*

Poculum Amatorium

The Romans called a love potion *poculum amatorium, the love cup.* In its most sublimated sense, the philtre contained "divin herbes."

Poetic Advice

Nefzawi, discussing amatory excesses in *The Perfumed Garden,* adds,

Having thus treated of the dangers which may occur from the coitus, I have considered it useful to bring to your knowledge the following verses, which contain hygienic advice in their respect. These verses have been composed by the order of Haroun er Rachid by the most celebrated physician of his time, whom he had asked to inform him of the remedies for successfully combating the ills caused by coition.

Eat slowly, if your food shall do you good, And take good

193

care, that it be well digested. Beware of things which want hard mastication. They are bad nourishment, so keep from them. Drink not directly after finishing your meal, Or else you go half way to meet an illness. Keep not within you what is of excess, And if you were in most susceptible circles, Attend to this well before seeking your bed, For rest this is the first necessity. From drugs and medicine keep well away, And do not use them unless very ill. Use all precautions proper, for they keep Your body sound, and are the best support. Don't be too eager for round-breasted women. Excess of pleasure soon will make you feeble, And in coition you will find a sickness. And before all beware of aged women, For their embraces will to you be poison. Each second day a bath should wash you clean; Remember these precepts and follow them.

See *PERFUMED GARDEN*.

Poetic Elixir

In his play *Volpone*, Ben Jonson presents the dwarf Nano singing the praises of an elixir that restores vigor and virility,

> You that would last long, list to my song,
> Make no more coil, but buy of this oil.
> Would you be ever fair and young?
> Stout of teeth, and strong of tongue?
> Tart of palate? quick of ear?
> Sharp of sight? of nostril clear?
> Moist of hand? and light of foot?
> Or, I will come nearer to't,
> Would you live free from all diseases?
> Do the act your mistress pleases,
> Yet fright all aches from your bones?
> Here's a medicine for the nones.

Poison Plants

The most virulent plants are those that contain alkaloids as active principles. Some of the alkaloids form active

194

principles in certain aphrodisiac compounds. Such compounds are generally fatal in their effects.

Polignonia

Also known as *Corrigiola* or *Alchone*. A herb whose juice is a potent aphrodisiac, according to Albertus Magnus (ca. 1206-1280), *De Secretis Mulierun.*

Pomegranate

According to Pliny the Elder, the Roman encyclopedist, the pith of the pomegranate tree was conducive to sexual activity.

Pork in Milk

Although pork itself is rarely mentioned as an amatory stimulant, this dish is credited with some rejuvenating virtue.

Porta, John Baptista

A Neapolitan writer. In his *Natural Magic,* published in English in 1658, he describes the preparation of Cyprian Powder and aphrodisiac aromatics.

In Book 9 he deals with feminine wiles and guiles, hair preparations, adornments, the art of decking themselves, painting of the face with the purpose, as Porta declares, of making themselves fair and beautiful to entice men.

Other subjects treated are, coloring of the hair—black or yellow, depilatories, changing the color of the eyes, soaps, dentrifrices, whitening of the cheeks, salt and sage as aids in heightening amatory allure, also comments on aphrodisiac and sexual matters, e.g., the salt meats used by the Egyptians to stimulate desire.

Potato

Although the potato actually has no exciting value, it was believed, in the seventeenth century, to possess definite aphrodisiac qualities, and is frequently mentioned in this respect in Elizabethan dramas.

In Shakespeare's *The Merry Wives of Windsor* reference

is thus made to the potato (which means the sweet potato),
Let the sky rain potatoes
And again,
How the devil luxury with his fat rump and potato finger tickles these together!
The allusion here is to lechery and lust so stimulated.

Potent Recipe

Brillat-Savarin, the famous French writer on gastronomy, recommends the potency of this dish,

an old rooster, ground, beef, parsley, turnips. All cooked separately, then mixed together and boiled once more.

Potions

Love potions, though effective, could also be highly dangerous and actually lead to death. In both ancient and medieval times such potions were often administered to lovesick girls, frenzied women, elders, and others whose *libido* or *voluptas* required stimulus.

St. Jerome, for instance, relates that the Roman poet Lucretius was poisoned by a love philtre.

On occasion, the potion was believed to affect the mind. In his *Remedium Amoris*, an erotic poetic manual, the poet Ovid says,

Philtres that cause pallor of the complexion are worthless for young women. They disturb the balance of the mind and light the fires of frenzied madness.

But the urge for sexual activity was often so desperate that the potential and frequently actual hazards associated with potions were completely disregarded.

Lucullus, the Roman general who flourished in the first century B.C., and who was also a famous gourmet, was rendered unconscious, according to the Greek biographer Plutarch and the Roman Cornelius Nepos, by drinking love potions.

It was also said that the Roman Emperor Caligula was

thrown into a fit by a potion given him by his wife Caesonia. She had intended the drink as a stimulating aphrodisiac.

The administration of love potions in Rome became so involved in criminal acts that Imperial decrees periodically made the giving of a love potion a punishable offense, on occasion, even subject to the capital penalty.

Power of Aphrodite

Aphrodite inspires men and women with the love craving, but she also satisfies them with her favors and gifts, power, wealth, beauty. She is however, innocent of any scruples whatever, moral or social. Passion overrides all. This concept of infatuation dominating all other feelings is well illustrated by the incidents that form the bulk of ancient mythology, Helen's passion for Paris, Medea's frenzy for Jason, forgetting parents, brothers, sisters, home, and friends, Ariadne, abandoned mistress, Pasiphae, writhing in unnatural lust, Phaedra, illicitly driven to her stepson Hippolytus.

Power of Love

In one of his poems Theocritus, the Greek poet, declares,

There is no other remedy against love, Nicias, it seems to me, neither salve nor plaster, but only the Muses.

The implication is that the only anti-aphrodisiac procedure is to occupy oneself wholeheartedly in some mental or occupational activity.

Longus of Lesbos, also a Greek writer, says,

Against love there is no remedy, neither a potion, nor powder, nor song, nothing except kisses, fondling, and *in puris naturalibus societate amoris coniungi.*

Prawns

The aphrodisiac nature of prawns is evident in an epigram by the Greek poet Asclepiades,

For a meal with a courtesan a purchase is to be made at

the market of three large and ten small fish and twenty-four prawns.

Prema Sagra
The Ocean of Love. A Hindu erotic manual translated into English late in the nineteenth century.

Premna Spinosa
Hindu erotology recommends, as provocative of amatory vigor, a drink composed of the following ingredients, Pounded fruits of the premna spinosa plant, asparagus racemosus, and the shvadaustra plant, boiled in water.

Priapeia
A collection of obscene Latin poems dealing with sexual acts and with the phallus as the pervasive motif.

See *PRIAPUS*.

Priapus
In ancient mythology, Priapus is the divinity whose symbol is the phallus. He is the son of Dionysus and Aphrodite and represents the physical crude principle of Eros. The goose, reputed to possess high generative power, was sacred to Priapus.

Priapus appeared as the leading character in an ancient comedy, and was often represented on the stage.

On coins from Lampsacus, on the Hellespont, he is shown in ithyphallic attitude.

In Roman times his cult was celebrated in special shrines, in rural communities, and among fishermen and sailors.

Priapus was frequently represented sculpturally, as a kind of scarecrow among the fields and even as a protection over graveyards.

Priests of Cybele
Cybele, the Mighty Mother of the Gods, had a cult that was associated with the woods and hills. Lions and panthers were her attendants, and frenzied priests her devotees. They

roamed the mountainsides and forests, creating din and clamor with horns and drums, pipes and castanets, and in their excitements they wounded and castrated themselves. This was a form of masochism that found sexual satisfactions in inflicted pain.

Priscianus Theodorus

A physician of the fourth century A.D. who advised, as a remedy for lack of sexual vigor,

Let the patient be surrounded by beautiful girls or boys, also give him books to read, which stimulate lust and in which love stories are insinuatingly treated.

Private Editions

Many manuals, poems, and dissertations of various kinds, dealing with sexual and aphrodisiac subjects, have been, particularly during the last century, privately printed, in limited editions, in London, Paris, Brussels, Benares, and elsewhere, for bibliophiles and other interested subscribers alone.

Among such editions may be included the *Kama Sutra*, *The Scented Garden*, *The Book of Exposition*, *L'Oeuvre Priapique des Anciens et des Modernes*, *The Bah-Nameh* of the Turkish Abdul-Hagg Effendi.

Proto-Historic Sexuality

In prehistoric times sexual faculties were symbolized by tribal ritual dances. These dances were based on the primary urges of ancient man, his need for food, and, by consequent implication, the need for fertility and procreation. The acquisition of food by the procreation of herds affected the nature of the ritual performances, injecting into them the basic sexual theme. In the course of time the dance rites, involving fertility in the widest sense, acted as aphrodisiac though indirect inducements to the entire tribe. The culminations of such rites, however, were entirely erotic, associated with prolonged sexual orgies.

Provincia

Called by the Chaldeans *Iterisi*. A herb that, when used in food, acts as an aphrodisiac on both men and women. Albertus Magnus (ca. 1206-1280), *De Secretis Mulierum*.

Provinsa

Called by Albertus Magnus *Provincia*.
See *PROVINCIA*.
Considered in the Middle Ages as the most powerful herb for inducing love. Identified with the Greek *Vorax*.

Psychological Aphrodisiacs

In many cases where there are no organic lesions or injuries, psychological influences have a direct bearing on erotic and sensory stimuli.

Psychological Treatment for Impotence

An Arab technique was for the physician—priest to place his hand over a goblet of water and recite a passage from the Koran for apotropaic purposes. The suppliant washed, drank the water, prayed, and made a digital contact with his genitals. The physician then recited the last two chapters of the Koran and sent the inquirer away hopefully. If this treatment proved ineffective, it was repeated three times at weekly intervals.

Public Chapels

In medieval towns there were still, in certain areas of Europe, devotees who paid homage to the antique god Priapus. They came as suppliants suffering from maladies associated wih the god's attributes. Images were offered to the deity, as well as reproductions of the genital parts that were affected. These offerings were in the form of paintings or figurines fashioned from wax, wood, or marble.

The women, too, offered garlands of flowers to the deity.

Pudenda Muliebria

Depilation of these organs was practised scrupulously in

ancient times. Aristophanes, the Greek comedy writer, makes amusing reference to this fact. During the Turkish Sultanate, it was a common practice among the harem women.

The object was to provoke the amatory inclinations of their partners.

Pulleiar
The Hindu erotic double symbol representing the lingam and the yoni. The pulleiar was venerated by the worshippers of Siva, one of the triune deities of India.

Purslane
A succulent herb found near water. Used in salads.

Also believed to act as an anti-aphrodisiac and so used for that purpose.

Pursuit of Pleasure
Man's frank and ceaseless pursuit of sensual pleasure has made him roam the earth and scour the seas, and has brought under contribution, as attendants on his amatory impulses, both naturally growing things—plants and shrubs, but also animal matter and deadly or scatological ingredients. With the advance of knowledge, too, and scientific techniques, synthetic compounds have been perfected, directed toward similar ends.

The results, in general, are that man often achieves the sensual stimuli desired, but at the grim expense of health, mental balance, and not infrequently life itself.

Pyrethrum
In ancient times pyrethrum parthenium, or pellitory, was used medicinally.

Among Arabs, when pyrethrum was pounded and mixed with ginger and lilac ointment, the compound was used, as a stimulant, to massage the lower genital area.

To the Greeks, pyrethrum—or pyrethron—was the plant that "kindles the flames of love."

Q

Quince Jelly
Reputedly, this jelly has a decided erotic effect.

Qualities of Phosphorus
Among instances that seem to establish the aphrodisiac qualities of phosphorus are these,

A drake belonging to a chemist, having drunk water out of a copper vessel which had contained phosphorus, continued its amorous activities until death.

An old man to whom a few drops of phosphoric ether had been administered experienced repeated and imperious venereal wants.

Two French physicians, in the eighteenth century, named Leroy and Battatz, tried the effects of phosphorus on themselves, with similar results.

The administration of phosphorus, however, even in small doses, has been productive, on the other hand, of the most horrible and fatal results.

Quinine
Quinine, taken in the evening, is considered by the Persians as an aphrodisiac aid.

R

Radishes

Radishes, beans, peas, and lentils were once popular in Germany in the belief that they were coital aids.

Radishes in particular were held in such high esteem as to warrant a poem. Entitled *Raporum Encomium*—Eulogy of Radishes—this glorification was published in Latin in 1540, in Lyons. It is still extant. The author was a certain Claude Bigothier.

Radix Chinae

A plant to which, both anciently and in medieval times, aphrodisiac qualities were ascribed.

Rakta-Bol

The Hindu name for myrrh. Powdered rakta-bol, costus arabicus, manishil, borax, and aniseed are mixed in oil of sesame. The ointment is then applied to the *membrum virile*.

Rambach

Author of an erotic anthology entitled *Thesaurus Eroticus Linguae Latinae*. Published in Stuttgart, in 1833.

Rauwiloid

Also known as *reserpine*. A drug used to reduce high blood pressure. It also produces erotic dreams, with some aphrodisiac effects.

The drug is extracted from the dried root of *Rauwolfia Serpentina*. This plant has been used in India for thousands of years for all kinds of illness, commonly as a headache remedy. In Sanskrit the plant is known as sarpagandha, which signifies *insanity cure*. The plant was named after Leonhard Rauwolf, a sixteenth century German horticulturist. *Serpentina* refers to the snaky roots of the plant.

The active principle, *rauwolfia*, is extracted from the powdered roots.

The dried root was chewed by holy men of India as an aid in contemplation. Mahatma Gandhi used it regularly.

The plant also grows in the Philippines, China, Java, and South America. In Guatemala it is known botanically as *Rauwolfia Heterophylla* and is natively called *chalchapa*.

Ray

It is claimed that this fish tends to increase seminal fluid.

See *FISH*.

Recipe with Cloves

Pounded cloves, to which milk is added, are recommended by an Italian erotologist.

Refrigerants

Refrigerants are medicines whose purpose is to produce anti-aphrodisiac effects. Among such preparations are infusions of leaves or flowers of the white water-lily—nymphea alba—, sorrel lettuce, mallows, violets, and endive. Also oily seeds. Another treatment involved water distilled from lettuce, water-lily, cucumbers, purslane, and endives. Also syrup of orgeat, lemons, vinegar, and cherry-laurel water.

Syrup of orgeat was a cooling potion, originally made from barley, later, from almonds, and orange-flower water.

According to Pliny the Elder, the Roman encyclopedist, author of the *Historia Naturalis,* nymphea alba was considered so powerful that those who took it for twelve days in succession found themselves incapable of propagating their species. If it was used for forty days, the amorous propensities, according to the same authority, would be entirely extinguished.

Rejuvenating Recipe

A Hindu love manual recommends a lotion consisting of juice of the roots of the madayantaka plant, yellow amaranth, anjanika plant, the clitoria ternateea, and the shlakshnaparni plant.

Rejuvenating Treatments

Within recent years laboratory experiments, glandular preparations, injections of hormones, and surgical operations involving transplantations have all been contributary toward inducing or rectifying sexual conditions.

But all such practices are of rigidly professional medical and surgical import.

Rejuvenation

As in the case of sexual virility and its diminution, the problem of senile rejuvenation is age-old. Even mythologically, the ancient witch Medea rejuvenated the aged Aeson by magic rites, boiling him in potent herbs.

Modern experimentation along the lines of rejuvenation is associated with Brown-Séquard, Voronoff, Steinach, and Ruzicka.

In a popular direction, this passion for acquiring rejuvenating vigor is evident in drug store advertisements in the United States. These announcements offer special preparations that are at least putatively directed toward the required purpose.

In Britain, the same kind of search is evidently proceeding. A popular weekly contains an advertisement of a similar type of prescription,

JENASOL RJ FORMULA 50. The Royal Jelly Rejuvenating Food supplement with 35 vitamins and Nutritional health builder now obtainable in capsule form.

Reptiles

Among the Romans, used as aphrodisiacs.

205

Reputation of Radishes

Radishes, mixed with honey, made a concoction that was commonly used by the Egyptians in the fifth century B.C.

Resin

All kinds of resins were used by the ancient Greeks and Roman as aphrodisiac ingredients.

Reputation of Monks

In the Middle Ages, the reputation of monks for lubricity and gluttony is illustrated in a Latin couplet that, translated, runs,

> Three things to ruin monks combine—
> Venery, gluttony, and wine.

Restoration of Virility

The Roman novelist Petronius describes, in his Satyricon, an ancient method of virile restoration,

Then the old woman took a twist of threads of different colors out of her dress, and tied it round my neck. Then she mixed some dust with spittle, and took it on her middle finger, and made a mark on my forehead despite my protest.

After this she ordered me in a rhyme to spit three times and throw stones into my bosom three times, after she had said a spell over them, and wrapped them in purple, and laid her hands on me and began to test the power of the groins.

Immediately the nerves obeyed her command and filled the hands of the old beldame with a huge flow. But triumphantly joyful she cried, "You see, my dear Chrysis, you see that I have aroused desire."

Rice

According to Hindu erotology, an effective sexual prescription runs as follows, A drink made from sparrows' eggs and rice, boiled in milk, to which are added honey and ghee.

The Hindu *Ars Amatoria*, the *Ananga-Ranga*, gives this prescription for erotic potency,

Wild rice mixed with honey of equal weight. Eaten in the evening.

In Britain too rice is reputed to increase the sexual faculties.

Rice Oil

This yellowish oil is obtained from the fresh leaves of a plant called *ruta graveolens*. Its effect is similar to that of cantharides, but somewhat milder in action.

See *CANTHARIDES*.

Riviere

A sixteenth century French physician, who offers the following formula for a potion,

Take of amber half a drachm, musk, two scruples, aloes, one drachm and a half, pound them all together, pour upon the mass a sufficient quantity of spirits of wine so that the liquor may cover it to the height of about five fingers' breadth; expose it to sand heat, filter and distill it, close it hermetically, and administer it in broth in the dose of three or five drops. This liquor is also advantageous when mixed with syrup, prepared as follows,

Take of cinnamon water, four ounces, orange and rose water, each six ounces, and a sufficient amount of sugar candy.

Rocket

A species of cabbage that grows in the Mediterranean region, used in salads. Reputed to be an aphrodisiac. Mentioned by the Roman poet Horace in this connection. Martial, too, the Roman epigrammatist, refers to it along with other aphrodisiacs,

> Scallions, lustful rockets nought prevail,
> And heightening meats in operation fail;
> Thy wealth begins the pure cheeks to defile,

207

So venery provoked lives but a while;
Who can admire enough, the wonder's such,
That thy not standing stands thee in so much?

Rocket, which is brasica eruca, possessed, according to the ancients, the virtue of restoring vigor to the genitalia. Hence it was consecrated to Priapus, and also sown around the sites of his statues.

In this regard, Columella, the Roman bucolic poet, says,

Th'eruca, Priapus, near thee we sow
To rouse to duty husbands who are slow.

Rocket Salad

Seasoned with olive oil, vinegar, pepper, and chopped garlic. Recommended by the Roman poets Ovid, Martial, and Columella. Ovid calls rockets salacious. Martial says that they invigorate amorous desire.

See *ROCKET*.

Roe

Cod and herring roe are considered high in aphrodisiac potential.

Roman Aphrodisiacs

A list of such items appears in the poet Ovid's *Ars Amatoria*, Book 2,

There are some who advise taking the noxious herb savory; in my judgment it is poison. Or they mix pepper with the seed of prickly nettle and yellow pellitory pounded in old wine. But the goddess whom lofty Eryx holds on his shady mount does not let herself thus be forced to her joys. Let white onions be taken, that are sent from the Pelasgian city of Alcathous, and the salacious herb that comes from the garden, and eggs, and Hymettian honey, and the nuts that the sharp-leaved pine brings forth.

Roman Enticements

To increase amatory advances, the Romans frequented

baths regularly and often. Pastilles were eaten to perfume the breath. Oils, pomades, and unguents were also brought under contribution, as well as rouge, creams, and preparations for the cheeks, hair, teeth, and nails.

An ancient writer describes the procedures in use,

They beautify their skin with an array of cosmetics . . . each maid carries something, a silver jar, a phial, a mirror . . . to polish the teeth or blacken the eyebrows and lashes . . . The lady dips her hair in henna to redden it and dries it in the midday sun . . . Another lady thinks black hair becomes her . . . with steel tongs she forces her curls into shape.

Roman Mimes

These ancient, silent, symbolic performances were acted out invariably by males. The mimes were packed with lascivious gestures and movements, and usually presented erotic scenes, on occasion farcically treated.

The themes regularly dealt with amorous intrigue, deceived wives, adulterous matrons, lovers disrupting domesticity, and similar situations in the mythological realms as well.

A characteristic of the mime was the uninhibited style of dancing of the performers. The effects on spectators were highly erotic.

Roman Technique

Every act of a Roman, from birth to death, from dawn to night, was controlled and supervised by some presiding deity. Man was thus virtually a symbolic puppet in the hands of the Roman pantheon. Human failings, errors, or weaknesses, both mental and physical, could be corrected or redressed only by adequate supplication to the proper divinities. Thus, in the case of lack of virility, the Romans made special invocations and performed *ad hoc* incantations in their suppliant appeals to the gods. This practice was prevalent throughout all Roman life. And if amatory competence resulted, particular thanks were duly and gratefully offered to the beneficent deity.

Roman Theatre
The Roman theatre was notorious as a place of debauchery. Isidore of Seville, a seventh century scholar and churchman, says,

Idem vero theatrum, idem et postibulum, eo quod post ludos exactos meretrices ibi prosternerentur.

Theatre and brothel were synonymous, for after the plays were over, the prostitutes there gave themselves to the public.

The Latin historian Livy similarly refers to the custom.

Romantic Aphrodisiac
The *Kama Sutra*, Hindu love manual, contains the following prescription,

Cut into small pieces the sprouts of the vajnasunhi plant, dip into a mixture of red arsenic and sulphur, dry seven times. Burn this powder at night and observe the smoke. If a golden moon is visible behind the fumes, the amatory experience will be successful.

Roman View of Sex
The sole object of the Roman marriage was to produce children to succeed their parents. Otherwise, according to the Roman historian Tacitus, the Roman married without love.

Rompini
In his *La Cucina dell'Amore* Omero Rompini mentions, as Italian items conducive to sexual activity, calves' testes, crayfish, truffles, carp, eels.

Rowlands
Samuel Rowlands, seventeenth century English dramatist,

gives a recipe for making an aphrodisiac powder of turtle-dove, to arouse love in the woman who takes the potion,

Take me a turtle-dove
And in an oven let her lie and bake
So dry that you may powder of her make;
Which, being put into a cup of wine,
The wench that drink'st it will to love incline.

Royal Senility

For Louis XIV's advancing age, a drink consisting of sugar, distilled spirits, and orange water was recommended as a restorative of vigor.

Rue

Like the water lily, endive, and lettuce, rue was believed to have anti-aphrodisiac properties.

S

Sacredness of Phallus

The sacredness of the phallus, in connection with the taking of an oath, is well attested in Northern European mores. An ancient law, enacted by the Welsh King Hoel the Good, contains, in the Latin text, a reference to this custom that dates back to Biblical times.

In the case of an assault on a woman, the woman could prosecute the offender. She must, however, according to the ancient Latin text, when swearing to his identity, lay her right hand upon the relics of the saints, and with her left hand grasp the membrum of the accused.

In more recent times it is recorded that among the London costermongers of the Victorian age a common oath, probably misunderstood or not understood at all, was, So help me testes!

Safflower

A thistle-like plant. In the fourth century it was highly recommended as a sexual stimulant.

Saffron

According to ancient legend, a Greek girl, partaking of saffron for an entire week, could not resist a lover. The reputation of saffron as an aphrodisiac has not wholly disappeared, although it is now used largely as a condiment in food.

A concoction consisting of saffron, orange blossoms, dried dates, anise, wild carrots, and egg yolk, boiled in clear water into which honey and the blood of two freshly killed doves have been poured, is recommended by Arabs as a sexual inducement.

Sage
A plant whose aromatic leaves are used for culinary purposes.

The juice, mixed with honey, is used for strengthening the voice and as a throat gargle. Sage also has a reputed stimulating value.

Salads
At various times and in different areas salads, compounded of meats, spices, tubers have been treated as of aphrodisiac value.

Among these are, A salad of tulip bulbs, tomato salad—the tomato often being assumed to be a love-apple, salad consisting of vinegar, garlic, salt and animal testes.

Salep
A jelly-like preparation made from the dried root of the orchis morio, which is the Turkish satyrion. Used in the Middle East formerly as a drug, also as a food.

In Turkey, Iran, and Syria salep is popular as a restorative and also as a provocative to amatory activity.

Salerno
In the medieval medical school of Salerno in Italy there was a widespread maxim in relation to the use of camphor,

> Camphora per nares
> castrat odore mares.
> Camphor if smell'd
> A man will geld.

Modern authorities however deny this property of camphor.

Camphor, however, has been used to counteract the conditions arising from nymphomania.

Salles De Préparations

Preparation-rooms, virtually laboratories, in which, in the eighteenth century in France, all sorts of concoctions and mechanical devices for the furtherance of sexual voluptuousness were developed.

Salmacis

A fountain in ancient Greece whose waters were reputed to produce effeminacy.

Salmon

Reputed to have high aphrodisiac value.

Salvia

A genus to which the plant sage belongs. Used for garnishing, also of aphrodisiac repute.

Samayamatrika

An Indian erotic manual by Kshemendra. Similar in intent and contents to the *Kama Sutra*.

See *KAMA SUTRA*.

Sandix Ceropolium

In ancient times this plant was credited with exciting amorous propensities. Tiberius, the dissolute Roman Emperor, is said to have exacted a certain quantity of the herb from the Germanic tribes, as tribute.

According to Dr. Venette, too, it was used in Sweden to encourage husbands in their matrimonial functions.

See *VENETTE*.

Sanseviera

A Hindu formula for sexual stimulus is a compound of the seeds of the plant sanseviera roxburghiana, long pepper, and the seeds of the plant hedysarum gangeticum, pounded together and mixed with milk.

Santonin

A drug once used as an aphrodisiac.

It is extracted from the dried flower heads of the plant

214

Artemisia maritima. Artemisia was so named after Queen Artemisia, wife of King Mausolus, who reigned in the fourth century B.C. The plant grew abundantly on hills and valleys, near the frontiers of Turkestan. Nomadic tribes used the herb for medicinal purposes. Other tribal groups, Mongolian and Kurdish, spread acquaintance with the plant East and West. In the West, it is cultivated in the south of England, near the sea and among the marshes.

As an aphrodisiac, it results in santonin poisoning, followed by coma and death.

Sardanapalus

An inscription on a stone statue of the ancient Assyrian King Sardanapalus emphasizes the zestfulness of his own epitaph, I have been a king and as long as I saw the light of the sun I have eaten, drunk, and done homage to the joys of love.

The inscription runs along the same lines,

Sardanapalus, the son of Anacyndaraxes, who conquered Anchiale and Tarsus on a single day. Eat! Drink! Love! for all else is naught.

Satureia

The plant savory, used by the Romans for aphrodisiac purposes.

See *SAVORY*.

Satyriasis

A condition involving intense and excessive amatory tendencies. The expression is associated with satyr. The satyrs, in the ancient mythology, were half goat, half human attendants of the god Pan. Their primary characteristic was unbridled lustfulness.

An early physician, a certain Baldassar Timoeus, describing the condition of salacitas, adds that a preparation of nitre, dissolved in aqua nymphea, cured a chronic case of satyriasis.

215

Satyrion

An obscure, unidentifiable plant, probably similar to the orchis. Known to the Greeks and Romans as a powerful aphrodisiac. The plant has smooth red leaves and a double root, the lower part of which is believed to be helpful in conceiving males, the upper part, females. According to some authorities, satyrion is akin to the Iris florantina. Also called Serapias. Serapias has pear-shaped leaves, a tall stem, and a root consisting of two tubers having the appearance of testicles.

The root was dissolved in goat's milk, and the reaction was so potent that, according to the historian Theophrastus, it produced on one occasion seventy consecutive acts of coitus.

Another species of satyrion was called erithraicon. If held in the hand, the plant provoked desire. To make the erotic desire subside, lettuce was eaten.

In ancient mythology, the efficaciousness of satyrion is attested, particularly in the case of Hercules. Pliny the Elder, the Roman encyclopedist, declares that its power to arouse sexual excitement is common knowledge. Petronius, the Roman novelist, also refers to the plant in his *Satyricon,* "We saw in the chambers persons of both sexes, acting in such a way that I concluded they must all have been drinking satyrion."

Again, "So saying, she brought me a goblet full of satyrion and with jests and quips and a host of marvelous tales induced me to drink up nearly all the liquor."

Satyrs

In Greek mythology, spirits of the woods. Half animal, usually in the form of a goat, and half human. They are the attendants of the rustic god Pan. The satyrs are characterized by bestiality and lust, and represent the elemental sexual passions of man.

Sauces

Many sauces have become widely popular because their

ingredients contain sexually stimulating spices and herbs. So with goose-liver preparations, mushroom sauces, and similar nutritive and at the same time aphrodisiac dishes.

Sauterne
Some connoisseurs believe that this wine has erotically stimulating effects.

Savory
A perennial used for seasoning. Aromatic and hot-flavored.

Formerly cultivated for its aphrodisiac properties. This herb—satureia, was well known to the ancient Romans, particularly the poet Ovid, as a sexual stimulant.

Scammony
A gum resin indigenous to the Middle East. Used in medicine. Compounded with honey, scammony is recommended as an aphrodisiac by Avicenna.

See *AVICENNA*.

Scatological Ingenuity
A startling fact in erotic literature is the amazing number of variants ingeniously devised, in the course of the ages, for certain amatory practices, anatomical areas, and similar items of venereal interest. Such practices are manifest both in the Orient and in the West. A notable instance is chapter 11 of *The Perfumed Garden,* in which Nefzawi lists some forty expressions for the pudenda muliebria.

Rabelais offers similar enumerations in his *Gargantua et Pantagruel.*

See *PERFUMED GARDEN*.

Scoptophilia
A synonym for voyeurism.
See *VOYEURISM*.

Seal of the Snake
A stone that, according to Moslem lore, was extracted

from a snake's head. It was commonly used as a love charm.
See *REPTILES*.

Sea-Slug

Found commonly off West Indian islands. Known widely
for its efficacious aphrodisiac virtues. Among the fishermen
of Naples, it is called *sea Priapus*.

Sedative Drugs

The organic hypnotics and the barbiturate drugs produce
an anaphrodisiac effect.

On the other hand, the bromides and, in some cases,
opium taken in some doses, may act in an aphrodisiac direction.

Semen

Used in magic rites, among the Romans, as an ingredient
in aphrodisiac concoctions.

Seneca

This Roman philosopher and tutor to the Emperor Nero
says, in his drama *Octavia*, that love is a mental condition,
fostered by leisure.

The same view has been held by sexologists from the
Middle Ages onward. Leisure, in fact, has been considered
a direct stimulus toward sexual inclinations.

Seneca's own words are as follows,

Love is a mighty force of the mind, and a gentle mental
heat, produced by youthful lust, nourished by idleness
amidst the good things that life brings.

Sesame

In Hindu erotology a sexual stimulant is made as follows,
Outer covering of sesame seeds, steeped in sparrows' eggs
and boiled in milk, ghee, and sugar, also the fruits of the
kasurika plant and the trapa bispinosa. Beans and flour
of wheat are then added. The concoction forms a drink,

Seventeenth Century Aphrodisiacs

In his *Tableau de l'Amour Conjugal,* Dr. Nicolas Venette, a French physician, discusses, as aphrodisiac items common in his time; cocks' testes, milk, sweet wine, yolk of eggs, prawns, crayfish, beef marrow, garlic, artichokes, hippomanes, campion.

Sex in Comedy

In the ancient Greek comedies of Eupolis, Aristophanes, Alexis, Timocles, and Menander, sex is predominant. The erotic and aphrodisiac tone is persistent and marked, characterized by what is to contemporary concepts obscenities, the representation of the phallus, worn by the male actors, and extreme erotic freedom of speech.

Women were usually not present as spectators although they were not specifically forbidden. The hetairae were most probably present, as well as young boys. For all sexual matters were openly presented without distortions or ambiguities.

Sexual Attraction in the Bible

Biblical criteria of sexual seductiveness include a white skin, black hair, or henna-dyed, scarlet lips, a prominent nose, rosy temples, long straight neck, firm breasts, round thighs, an erect posture.

These standards correspond virtually to Arab ideals.

Sexual Deities

Among the ancient Romans, sex consciousness was so intense that, associated with various successive stages of cohabitation, beginning with the marriage ceremonial, were deities who supervised and sponsored the sexual rituals. Notable among such divinities were Prema, Subigus, Juno, Pertunda, each of whom had a specific assigned function in the entire amatory procedure. The most ancient of these deities, in proto-historic times, was one called Mutunus Tutunus.

Sexual Ethics

In the ancient Sanskrit epics describing the Golden Age of man, sexual union was prescribed for the sole purpose of begetting offspring.

Sexual Grades

In the *Laws*, the Greek philosopher Plato declares that the Greeks make three classifications of women, Courtesans, for pleasure, concubines, for daily personal service, and married women to bear children and manage the house faithfully.

Sexual Hospitality

The practice of offering a wife or other woman, for amatory purposes, to a guest or stranger, dates back into Biblical times. It is also characteristic of the Middle East in modern days, and of many tribes in Southern Arabia and in Oman. Yaqut, a fourteenth century Arab geographer, Ibn Battuta, the most distinguished Arab traveler, and, as late as the early nineteenth century, J.L. Burckhardt, who made an expedition to Mecca, all testify to this practice, which has actually a pre-Islamic tradition.

Shallot

A small onion, used in sauces and salads. Martial, the Roman epigrammatist, refers to its aphrodisiac value,

If envious age relax the nuptial knot, Thy food be scallions, and thy feast shallot.

See *ONIONS*.

Sheep

In Persia, newly married couples were presented with sheep's trotters steeped in vinegar as a love enticement.

Shell-Fish

All kinds of shell-fish were considered by the Greeks as aphrodisiacs. In modern times the same traditional belief prevails.

See *FISH*.

Showers

One Arab writer recommends cold showers, twice daily, and cold compresses as a cure for lack of sexual vigor. In Britain, cold showers are advised as an anaphrodisiac.

Shrimp

Most sea foods, particularly shrimps, have a wide-spread and traditional enticement for erotic encounters.

See *SHELL-FISH*.

Shunammitism

A practice prevalent, in Biblical and other times.

It involves visual, tactile, and clinical contacts of young girls by elders, in order to encourage or restore vigor.

A detailed description of the procedure, applied in the case of King David, appears in I Kings I. 1-4,

Now King David was old and stricken in years; and they covered him with clothes, but he gat no heat.

Wherefore his servants said unto him, Let there be sought for my lord the king a young virgin; and let her stand before the king, and let her cherish him, and let her be in thy bosom, that my lord the king may get heat.

So they sought for a fair damsel throughout all the coasts of Israel, and found Abinhag a Shunammite, and brought her to the king.

And the damsel was very fair, and cherished the king, and ministered to him; but the king knew her not.

So also in Ben Jonson's *Volpone*,
And since, to seem the more officious
And flatt'ring of his health, there, they have had,
At extreme fees, the College of Physicians
Consulting on him, how they might restore him;
Where one would have a cataplasm of spices,
Another a flayed ape clapped to his breast,
A third would have it a dog, a fourth an oil,
With wild cats' skins, at last, they all resolved

That, to preserve him, was no other means,
But some young woman must be straight sought out,
Lusty, and full of juice, to sleep by him;
And to this service, most unhappily,
And most unwillingly, am I now employed.

Roger Bacon, too, the medieval philosopher, discusses this practice from a scientific viewpoint.

Shvadaustra

For increasing sexual vigor, Hindu erotic manuals prescribe a drink composed of the following ingredients,

The shvadaustra plant, the guduchi plant, asparagus racemosus, liquorice, and long pepper, boiled in ghee, milk and honey. Taken in the spring time.

Sicinnis

A Greek erotic dance, representing the jumping of goats. It was associated with the sensual ways of satyrs.

See *SATYRS*.

Significance of Mandrake

Columella, the Roman bucolic poet who flourished in the first century A.D., calls mandrake vesanus, *maddening*, because it was in his time believed to form an ingredient in love-potions that were intended to drive the victim mad.

In the Middle Ages quacks and mountebanks often played on the credulity of the ignorant populace at fairs and markets by exhibiting little rudely-carved figures that they claimed to be mandrakes.

John Wierus, the sixteenth century demonographer, exposes the procedure in the monumental monograph on witchery, *De Praestigiis Daemonum et incantationibus ac Veneficiis*. He says,

Imposters carve upon these plants while yet green the male and female forms, inserting millet or barley seeds in

222

such parts as they desire the likeness of human hair to grow
on.

These objects are then sold, he adds, to credulous peasants
and love-sick men and maidens.

An old French chronicler comments on the repute,
wide and assured, that was enjoyed in the middle centuries
by mandrakes,

La racine et la branche
    de toute abusion.
Chef de l'orgueil du monde
    Et de lubricité.
The root and branch of every abuse.
Greatest pride in the world,
Height of lubricity.

La Fontaine, the French fabulist, has a tale, *La Mandragore,* dealing with the erotic impact of the root.

Significance of Sexual Power

In proto-historic times sexual potency was demonstrated
by ritual dances, organized and controlled by priests of the
ethnic community. The basic theme of these performances
was the fact of procreation, of human propagation. Hence
these ceremonial dances were designated, anthropologically,
as fertility rites.

Fertility was of such primary significance for the continued existence and perpetuation of a community that
techniques associated with sexual desire and amatory expression became vested, as a corpus of secretive knowledge,
in priest-magicians, sorcerers, occultists, witches.

When, in the Middle Ages, the question of sex became
ecclesiastically linked with Satanic and malefic motives, and
sex became "the handmaiden of the devil," the witch and
the warlock came into their own. What was forbidden assumed increased value, and the sexual stimulus went rampant. The witch, repository of hieratic lore and folk legends

and occult arcana, became the distributor of philtres and unguents, electuaries and pastilles, herbs and charms and incantations—directed toward sexual pleasures and amatory satisfactions.

Aphrodisiacs were not confined to any one geographical area, to any particular ethnic group, or to any one isolated cult. Aphrodisiacs, in their source and their purpose, permeated every continent, every century in a common objective whose consummation was sexual expression.

Granted the conditions of human life, hostilities and repulsions, bitter enmities, fears, and jealousies stirred the members of each community. Hence the desire to achieve dominance by inherent sexual potency or by such powers contrived through the aid and machination of adepts, magicians, witches, alchemists. On the other hand, it was equally the case that a personal enmity would compel a victim of such enmity to resort for help to the local beldame steeped in magic lore. The most effective way to crush an enemy was to deprive him of virility. Hence arose the search for anti-aphrodisiacs to be used on opponents, and the accumulations either by oral tradition or in transmitted written form of such negative and preventive operations.

Certain herbs, in the course of ages, acquired, in the popular mind, specific amatory properties, either in actuality, or by implication and suggestion. Exotic plants were brought for this purpose by travelers from distant lands. Spices reached Europe after being carried over the Asiatic caravan routes by the Radanite merchants, to be re-distributed among traders and apothecaries, pilgrims and princelings. These spices and herbs, these unique ointments and balsams, powders and potions came with stories and traditions of erotic manifestations attached to them. Herbalists began to classify such products and specify their particular properties. So sex-provoking powers were acquired by Cannabis and Hemlock, Satyrion and Yohimbine.

Siva

In Hindu mythology, the chief warden of the phallus.

Skink

Latin, scincus officinalis. A small lizard, indigenous to Arabia and North Africa. Formerly prized medicinally. Also once considered, and still treated in Arabia, as a potent aphrodisiac when it is fried in oil.

See *LIZARD*.

In the Antilles the skink is called *mahuiha* and *brochet terrestre*. Dr. Venette calls it the *little crocodile*.

See *VENETTE*.

Skirret

Nicolas Venette, French physician, refers to skirret, a plant that has esculent tubers, for its high aphrodisiac potential.

It was related of the Roman Emperor Tiberius that he had these plants imported from Germany in order to promote his sexual orgies.

See *VENETTE*.

Snails

The ancients considered them as aphrodisiacs. The Roman poets mention them in this respect.

A rejuvenating recipe, used in contemporary times, requires the following items,

Snails boiled with onions, parsley, and garlic, then fried in olive oil. Then boiled again in strong red wine.

Snuff

According to the Sheik Nefzawi, author of *The Perfumed Garden,* snuff, plain or scented, acts as an aphrodisiac.

See *PERFUMED GARDEN*.

Solitary Pleasures

Various lewd contrivances, among them the Chinese

'hedge-hog,' ovoid objects, and similar apparatus have all been perversely used as amatory stimulants. Such objects and practices date back into antiquity.

In Tientsin, Dr. Jacobus mentions that in 1860 gommo-resinous phalli were sold publicly in the streets. He also refers to a strange contraption used by debauched and senile Chinese.

See *JACOBUS*.

Song of Nala

Hindu epic poem that alludes to magic devices, spells, incantations to overcome sterility and stimulate sexual potency.

King Brihadratha, ruler of Magadha, although sunk in sensual pleasure, had no son. Magic charms and sacrifices being of no avail, he consulted the ascetic Candakaucika, who gave him a juicy mango that had just fallen from a tree. The King gave the fruit to his two wives. Each produced half a child. But the parts were finally brought together and a healthy male child was the result.

Songs

Songs, pervaded by erotic allusiveness, have from ancient antiquity onward been a characteristic factor at banquets and similar festivities.

The expression *Wine, Women, and Song* is no idle phrase. The truth of this apothegm is illustrated in universal literature, from the Greek Anacreon to the Goliardic chants of the Middle Ages and to the Oriental views of Omar Khayyam.

Sotades

A Greek poet of Maroneia in Crete, who lived in the third century B.C. His poems, most of which have meagrely survived in fragments, were marked by obscene scatological language and sexual themes. One of his poems, called *Pria-*

pus, was composed in a jocular vein and was dedicated to the primary function of the god.

See *PRIAPUS.*

Soup

Fish soup, in Hindu erotology, is assumed to have an aphrodisiac value.

Among stimulating soups are onion soup, cheese soup, lentil soup, mushroom soup, celery soup.

Southernwood

According to the Roman Pliny the Elder, author of *Historia Naturalis,* southernwood was conducive to sexual excitement when the plant was placed under the bed.

Southernwood also counteracted charms against conception.

Spargeus

The name of one of the mythological creatures known as Centaurs, partly human, partly equine. The Centaurs were associated with a cult on Mount Helicon. Spargeus itself means *lustful.*

Sparrow

Male sparrows were eaten to produce a heightened sexual awareness.

Spartans

In ancient Sparta girls practised gymnastic exercises if not naked, then so tightly clad as to provoke sensual excitement on the part of the male onlookers.

Sperm

Deer sperm was in use among the Romans as an aphrodisiac.

Spinach

Considered, on account of its rich iron content, as an amatory stimulant.

Spurge

A plant whose milky juice has medicinal virtue. A compound of spurge, cardamom, cinnamon of Mecca, pellitory, ginger, nettle seed is an Arab specific for sexual weakness.

Sterility

In the Orient in particular, but no less so in European and other countries, the disastrous condition of female sterility has for centuries been a primary inducement in the search for aphrodisiac aids.

St. Foutin

St. Foutin de Varailles, an early Christian saint associated with Provence. By some interchange of identity and through the obscurities of folk legends, St. Foutin was credited with the attributes of Priapus.

Wax models of the pudenda of both sexes were regularly placed before his altar. These objects were believed to have stimulating powers and to aid in the cure of amatory diseases and obscure maladies.

Libations were made to the image of the saint. The wine used in such libations was preserved later as holy vinegar and used for erotic purposes.

St. Ignatius' Beans

That is, strychnos ignatii, a plant that grows in the Philippine Islands. From this bean, early in the nineteenth century, strychnine was isolated.

A dangerous poison, formerly and erroneously mistaken as aphrodisiac in action, but it is fatal, and has no aphrodisiac value.

Stimulus of Dill

Anethum graveolens. Used in the East as an ingredient for arousing desire.

228

Stimulus of Wine

In one of the comedies of Aristophanes a youth exclaims,

O might I find, dear gods, my fair one alone, to whom I might hasten, flushed with wine and overcome with longing for her.

Storgethron

A plant used in Greece as a love medicine.

It has been identified with the common leek.

Stramonium

A plant whose botanical name is Datura Stramonium, the Thorn Apple. Called in Turkish Datoula. A narcotic drug is extracted from the plant. Largely used in the Orient.

Stramonium seed, mixed in wine, produces, according to a seventeenth century erotologist, libidinous activity. The effects, the writer asserts, are similar to those produced by bhang. Excessive consumption, however, may prove fatal.

See *BHANG*.

Strombus

Certain parts of a species of strombus, found in the Black Sea, were used among Somali women as an aphrodisiac, according to Dr. Jacobus X.

See *JACOBUS*.

Sturgeon Soup

The sturgeon is considered to be rich in aphrodisiac elements. In the Mediterranean area this is a very popular dish.

Surag

A root that was anciently regarded, according to Leo Africanus, as a powerful aphrodisiac.

Swallow Nest Soup

Popular in China for restoring exhausted potency.

229

Swan

The swan's genitals have been used in cooking as an aphrodisiac.

Symposia

In ancient Greece, the symposia were drinking parties, interlarded with literary and philosophical talk, and singing and dancing entertainments by both sexes. The Greek historian Xenophon and the philosopher Plato describe such gatherings, also the biographer Plutarch, and Athenaeus who flourished in the third century A.D. and produced a vast encyclopedia entitled *Banquet of the Philosophers.*

A popular forfeit at such banquets, was to dance naked or to carry the female flute-player three times round the room, a performance which usually ended in sexual diversions.

Often the guests, affected by the wine drinking, released all inhibitions and made erotic overtures, particularly to the slave cup-bearers.

Synonyms

Not only does Nefzawi, author of *The Perfumed Garden,* list numerous Arab synonyms for the membrum virile, but in eleven pages he discusses the peculiarities and significance of each name. After which he adds, I think I have given a nomenclature long enough to satisfy my readers.

See *PERFUMED GARDEN.*

Syrian Cult

In ancient Syria, Aphrodite's cult was marked by the dominance of the phallus. It was a symbol of the all-pervasive sexual life of its devotees.

T

Tabernamontana Coronaria

For erotic purposes, a Hindu manual suggests a powder composed of tabernamontana coronaria, costus arabicus, flacourtia cataphracta. Applied to the wick of a lamp that burns with oil of blue vitriol. The resultant black pigment or lamp black, applied to the eyelashes, has a seductive effect on the observer.

Tactile Aphrodisiacs

Aphrodisiac reactions often arise from mere touch of the body of the opposite sex, by means of contact of fingers, shaking of hands, or tongue proximity.

Tarragon

A plant indigenous to South Eastern Europe. The aromatic leaves of the plant are used to flavor salads. Reputed of aphrodisiac value.

Telephilon

Theocritus, an ancient Greek poet, says that the leaf of a flower called *telephilon* was used by the boys of Crotona as an amatory oracle. A leaf was placed in the palm of the hand or on the arm, and then struck sharply. A crackling sound, as a result, portended a good omen.

Telephilon has been identified as a kind of pepper tree, or, according to some, as the poppy.

Tempting Powder

In Obeah, the magic cult prevalent in the West Indies, and especially in Jamaica, a love philtre.

Terence

A Roman comedy writer of the second century B.C. In the course of his comic scenes, he belittles the amorous excitations by reference to the negative or unappealing aspects of love, including quarrels, suspicion, sudden indifference.

Tertullian

One of the Roman Fathers of the Church who belongs in the third century A.D. His attacks on pagan rites and beliefs include a general condemnation of Roman public festivals and entertainments as virtual sexual orgiastic stimulants. Public shows, to Tertullian, are a "gathering of the wicked." The Roman theatre is the shrine of Venus, licentious and unbridled. Venus and Bacchus, in conjunction, are demons of lust. The Roman theatre is packed with filth, in the gestures of the actors, in the words of the farces, in the motions of the buffoon who plays the part of a woman. All sense of sexual shame is banished. The very prostitutes, victims of the public lust, are brought on the stage . . . they are paraded before the faces of every rank and age . . . announcement is made of their dwelling, the fee they charge, their sexual reputation. Both tragedies and comedies teach outrage and lust, they are virtually and actually erotic excitements.

In his treatise on Women's Toilette, he makes a comprehensive attack on Roman women's enticing use of pomades, perfumes, oils, rouge, paste, ornamentation of hair, all deliberately directed toward the stimulation of men's sexual appetites.

Testes

In many countries, and under various circumstances, animal testicles were assumed to possess powerful sexual virtues. Alexandre Dumas, himself an excellent chef, usually recommended ram's testicles for such a purpose. So in Spain, Provence, and Tuscany.

In France, Mme. de Pompadour was induced by Louis

XV to eat such testicles in order to break down her frigidity.

In Morocco and Algeria the testicles of lion are similarly highly prized.

As the ass is known for its erotic activities, the testicles of this creature were commonly included in aphrodisiac recipes.

Testes of Lamb

These are recommended, for aphrodisiac reasons, by a famous Italian chef, Cartolomeo Scappi.

See *TESTES*.

Testicular Application

According to Galen, the second century A.D. Greek physician, the male genitalia are the second source of heat, which is communicated to the entire body. Applications therefore of concoctions to this area have been considered, as Davenport writes, of stimulant value. One erotologist declares that the best application of this kind is composed of cinnamon powder, gilliflower, ginger, and rose water, together with theriac, bread crumbs, and red wine.

Here the usual caveat must be entered.

Text on Sexology

The Elements of Social Science or Physical, Sexual and Natural Religion, with a Solution of the Social Problem. By a Doctor of Medicine. Published in London, by Edward Truelove, at 256 High Holborn.

An early text, in English, on sexological problems and their impact on society.

Theocritus

A Greek bucolic poet who flourished in the third century B.C. His poems are full of amorous situations, magic spells, and philtres.

Theophrastus

A third century B.C. Greek philosopher and writer. He mentions a plant brought from India with a peculiar property. Not only eating it, but the mere touch of the plant kindles desire and makes it possible to consummate the desire continuously. He says,

There was a herb that was remarkably effective in sexual activities. It had been imported by an Indian. It was said that, apart from eating the herb, the mere touch of it on the genitalia produced unending potency.

The herb, however, has not been identified.

Thesis

In 1695, at the Ecole de Médecine, in Paris, a thesis was presented maintaining that the daily use of coffee deprived both man and woman of the generative power.

Thread

Woolen threads were an occult means, according to the Roman poet Horace, of depriving a person of virility.

Thyme

This fragrant herb has been in use for medicinal purposes, as flavoring in cookery, and as an erotic stimulus.

Tincture

The tincture of the gold known as Mademoiselle Grimaldi's potable gold had a wide reputation in the eighteenth century as an aphrodisiac stimulant.

Toe

An old traditional prescription for provoking erotic inclinations ran as follows,

The toe of the foot of a man, anointed with oil, or honey, or the ashes of a weasel.

Tomatoes

Believed by some to have aphrodisiac value.

Tonka

A drug that has been considered to have aphrodisiac properties. It is obtained from the *Tonquin* beans, the ripe seeds of *Coumarouna odorata*. They have a fragrant aroma but are bitter to the taste. Tonka is used to flavor foods, and also as a mild aphrodisiac agent.

Tortoise

The tortoise, with its characteristic protrusion of the head and neck, was a symbol sacred to Venus. It represented the procreative principle.

Transvestism

A perversion that involves the donning of the dress of the opposite sex for the purpose of producing sexual excitement. This perversion is as old as ancient Greece, and was prevalent at the festival of Cotyttia in Thrace, Athens, and Corinth. The festival was associated with licentious mysteries, in the name of the goddess Cotys.

A certain governor of Babylon, named Amarus, used to appear in elaborate female dress.

The condition was known to the Romans too, and is mentioned by the poet Horace in connection with these sexual orgiastic rites.

At the sacrifices to the hermaphroditic god Aphroditos, men assumed female clothing and women wore male dress.

In Sparta, the bride assumed male dress and had her hair cut short. On the island of Cos, the bridegroom donned female dress. At Argos, too, at the annual festival of Hybristika, men and women wore the dress of the opposite sex. Behind such practices lies the ancient concept of the androgynous nature of life, that is, the dual functions and characteristics of male and female united in one body.

Lucian, the Greek satirist, represents an old pedant, Craton, rebuking an elderly philosopher,

What must anyone think of you, who have enjoyed a learned education, and have a moderate knowledge of philosophy, when you abandon the noblest studies . . . while you are looking at an effeminate man, who swaggers about in a soft female dress, and with most lustful songs and movements represents the most notorious women of antiquity. (Loeb Classical Library).

Modern "female impersonators" adopt the practice of transvestism for theatrical purposes.

Transvestism in Juvenal

Juvenal, the Roman satirist, when treating of the vices and perversions of degenerate Roman society, has violent and bitter things to say about the "imitation" women, the men who, in private clubs, assume female dress, powder their faces, use hair-nets, and in general ape female ways in a distorted erotic sense.

Trapa Bispinosa

A plant used in Hindu aphrodisiac concoctions.

A potent composition is the following,

Roots or seeds of the plants trapa bispinosa, tuscan jasmine, kasurika, and liquorice, and an onion-like bulb named kshirakapoli, powdered and mixed with sugar, milk, and ghee. The compound is then boiled and the resultant paste is taken as a beverage.

Botanically, trapa bispinosa is a nut of the same species as water chestnut. It is indigenous to India and Southern Europe.

Tribadism

This expression means homosexuality among women, commonly called Lesbianism.

The exponent of this aberration was the Greek poetess Sappho, who was born on the island of Lesbos in the seventh century B.C.

Her poetry was so sensual and filled with amatory imagery that Ovid, the Roman erotic poet, urgently recommended the reading of Sappho's poems to the Roman girls and women of his day.

236

Trimurti

In India, phallic worship is associated with Trimurti, the triune god.

Tripe

A popular dish commonly believed to be a sexual stimulant.

Triphallus

The name of a satire by the Roman satirist Varro. Triphallus itself means a person with three members. The erotic nature of the satire may be deduced from the title.

Trout

Roman matrons, sexually exhausted, were fond of trout caught in a little stream in the Vosges Mountains.
See *FISH*.

Truffles

The truffle is an edible fungus, indigenous to Europe. Known to the Romans. Long considered as a sexual inducement and used for stuffing game, etc. Napoleon was advised by one of his generals to eat truffles to increase potency. A French eulogy of truffles runs as follows,

> Buvons à la truffe noire;
> Et ne soyons point ingrats.
> Elle assure la victoire
> Dans les plus charmants combats.
> Au secours
> Des amours
> Du plaisir la Providence
> Envoya cette substance.
> Qu'on en serve tous les jours.
> Let's drink the health of truffles black;
> In gratitude we must not lack.
> For they assure us dominance
> In all erotic dalliance.

As an aid to lovers' bliss
Fate pleasurably fashioned this
Rarity, divine godsend,
To use for ever without end.

Turkish Recipe
One such recipe recommends Algerian truffles as an aid to sexual competence.
See *TRUFFLES*.

Turmeric
A substance derived from the curcuma, the saffron plant. Considered an efficacious stimulant.

Turnips
Stewed in a milk sauce, turnips have been medically recommended as helpful toward potency.

Turtle's Heart
A unique anti-aphrodisiac was the heart of a turtle carried in a wolf's skin. It prevented a person from ever being tempted amorously.

Tychon
An ithyphallic spirit associated with the goddess of love Aphrodite.

Tyrolean Custom
Among the peasants of the Tyrol, it is customary, during a dancing session, to hold a handkerchief under the armpit, later on, the dancer may give this handkerchief to a reluctant sweetheart, a folk way that is considered effective in inciting amatory responses in the girl.

Tyrrhenians
Among this ancient people maidservants waited upon the men naked. Sexual acts were promiscuous. The women, to preserve their physical beauty, practised gymnastics, together with men, *in puris naturalibus*.

U

Uchchata

The root of the Indian plant uchchata, piper chaba, and liquorice, mixed with sugar and steeped in milk, produce a beverage that is, in Hindu erotology, assumed to promote sexual vigor.

Unnatural Acts

A Chinese expression indicates the public awareness of the practice of perverted amatory manoeuvres. The term is Gik thien so hing, *to act contrary to the course of nature.*

Urid

Urid seeds are a kind of chick-pea or gram. Used in India as a common item of food.

The Hindu manual *Ananga-Ranga* recommends, for regaining amatory assertiveness, the following recipe,

Urid seeds steeped in milk and sugar. The mixture is left in the sun for three days, reduced to a powdery form, it is kneaded into cakes and fried in ghee. The cakes are eaten each morning.

Urination

Pliny the Elder, the Roman encyclopedist, declares that to urinate in a spot where a dog has previously done so results in loss of virility.

Urtication

A form of flagellation administered with fresh nettles.

This practice was well known in ancient times. It is mentioned, for example, by the Roman medical writer Celsus, who flourished in the first century A.D. The Romans had frequent recourse to urtication to arouse the sexual appetite. The Roman novelist and satirist, Petronius, author of the *Satyricon,* describes the treatment,

Oenothea semiebria ad me respiciens, "Perficienda sunt," inquit, "mysteria ut recipias nervos."

Simulque profert scorteum fascinum quod, ut olio et minuto pipere atque urticae trito circumdedit semine, paulatim coepit inserere ano meo. Subinde femina mea nasturcii succum cum abrotono miscet, perfusisque inguinibus meis, viridis urticae fascem comprehendit omnesque partes infra umbilicum coepit lenta manu caedere.

Use of Aphrodisiacs

In remote antiquity, throughout the Middle Ages, in contemporary society as well as currently among primitive tribes, the search for aphrodisiacs has always been, and continues to be, unending.

Aphrodisiac aids have included chemical preparations, animal compounds, plant extracts.

The quest for such amatory panaceas has always involved traditional lore and superstitious ceremonies. Obscure techniques and alluring quack remedies, appealing advertisements, charlatans' advice, cryptic formulas, exotic foods, drinks, and medicinal concoctions have all played their illusive but provocative part in presenting before hungry, perplexed, ignorant, or passionate men and women a final, complete, and effective solution to their emotional or psychic amatory ills.

Even when frustration or disappointment repeatedly occurs, the hope for the supreme aphrodisiac never falters. Hence every new or untried drug or philtre, powder or ointment or technique, however putative, baseless in its efficaciousness, becomes one more prop for the untired searcher.

Use of Perfume

In that remarkably comprehensive amatory guide, *The*

Perfumed Garden, Nefzawi has effective comments to make on the significance of perfumes in erotic situations. The woman, he declares, inhales the perfumes employed by the man and gets like into a swoon, and the use of scents has often proved a strong help to man, and assisted him in getting possession of a woman.

See *PERFUMED GARDEN.*

V

Vagaries of Women

Honoré de Balzac, the nineteenth century French novelist, says: On peut tout attendre et tout supposer d'une femme amoureuse.

From a women in love, anything may be expected and anything may be assumed.

Valerian

This herb has been used medicinally as a stimulant. It has also had some aphrodisiac reputation.

Van De Velde, Th.

Contemporary Dutch gynaecologist and sexologist who treats the subject of erotic cookery as of established medical value.

Vanilla

Universally considered a pleasant, aromatic aphrodisiac, although it is often innocuously used in flavoring foods. Its association with sexual activity stems from the fact that the word is a diminutive of the Latin term *vagina*.

Vanilla itself was transplanted from Madagascar, the main source of the spice, to Polynesia a century ago.

Madame de Pompadour was fond of chocolates spiced with vanilla and amber.

Vanilla Oil

Used as a base in perfumery. Vanilla itself, vanilla planifolia, produces an aromatic substance from the vanilla capsules. Used in flavoring, and once considered, by both gourmets and erotologists, as a powerful amatory stimulant.

Vatodbhranta

For erotic stimulus, a love manual suggests an application of a mixture of the leaf of the plant vatodbhranta, flowers thrown on a human corpse, the powder of peacock bones and of the jiwanjiva bird.

Veal Sweetbread

An occasional mention ascribes some sexual virtue in this dish.

Vegetable Extracts

The ancient Greeks and Romans were familiar with such extracts for provoking the sexual urge.

Venette

In the seventeenth century, a French physician, Dr. Nicolas Venette, published a *Tableau de l'Amour Conjugal,* in which he discusses sexual relationships and gives advice on remedies that are sexually stimulating as well as on means of controlling excessive amatory urges.

Venison

Medically recommended as a sexual stimulant.

Venus Fisica

In ancient Pompeii, Aphrodite was worshipped as the goddess that arouses and stimulates amatory passion. Fisica itself is etymologically associated with the Greek expression that means *genitalia.*

Venus Verticordia

Venus who turns hearts. In ancient Rome a shrine was dedicated to this divinity. The motive of the worship was to divert women from the customary debauchery toward chastity.

In this connection, in 114 B.C., three Roman priestesses, called officially Vestal Virgins, were condemned to death for sexual intimacies.

Venus Volgivaga

Venus the Streetwalker. A name of the deity Venus in her capacity as the patroness of harlots. A special festival in her honor was celebrated on April 23, according to the poet Ovid.

The Greek poet Theocritus refers to the same goddess as the Pandemic Cyprian divinity.

Vergil

Roman epic poet of the first century B.C. who also wrote a series of pastoral sketches in which he describes amorous encounters, magic love ceremonials, and philtres.

Virtues of Salt

Anciently, and in the Middle Ages, salt was believed to be an aphrodisiac. It was associated mythologically with the goddess Venus, the deity of love, who was said to have arisen from the sea.

Hence originated a widespread epigram,

In Venice why so many whores abound?
The reason sure is easy to be found,
Because, as learned sages all agree,
Fair Venus' birthplace was the salt, salt sea.

Virtue of Truffles

An erotologist declared that truffles were credited with "being a positive aphrodisiac, disposing men to be exacting, and women complying."

Visual Aphrodisiac

A popular dress among ancient Greek women was made of a fine flax that grew on the island of Amorgos, the clothes so fashioned being known as Amorgina. They were thin and transparent, clinging to the contours of the body. Silk fabrics were also favored, particularly those from the island of Cos, and ready-made garments of this material were imported from Assyria.

On one occasion, female flute-players who appeared at a wedding feast were thought by the guests to be completely unclothed, until it was explained that they were wearing Coan dresses.

Later, in Roman times, the novelist Petronius alludes to such dresses as "woven stuff light as air." Seneca, the tutor of the Emperor Nero, a Stoic philosopher and moralist, fulminates against such flimsy, revealing clothes that were actually erotic encouragements. "I see silken clothes, if those can be called clothes, with which the body or only the private parts could be covered; dressed in them, the woman can hardly swear with a good conscience that she is not naked. These clothes are imported at considerable expense from most distant countries, only that our women may have no more to show their lovers in the bedroom than in the street."

Like perfumes, all such deliberately devised robes made their subtle but distinctive and persistent amatory attack on men.

In the Museums of Europe, too, there are sculptural representations of the dual god Hermaphoditos in sexual embrace with the god Pan or with the Satyrs. All such visual erotic manifestations tended to add an aphrodisiac stimulus to the beholder.

In Greek mythology, the hunter Actaeon spied on the goddess Artemis as she was bathing among her nymphs. As a punishment, Actaeon was changed into a stag and torn to pieces by his own dogs.

A certain Siproetes, too was guilty of the same offense against Artemis. His punishment was to be turned into a woman.

245

In Rome a sculptural image of Hermes depicts him bending over toward an almost naked nymph, caressing her breast with one hand and pulling aside her flimsy garment.

Visual Attraction

Among some primitive tribes, the headdress of girls is capable of arousing sexual desire.

In some cases, photographs, sculptured pieces, shoes, various pieces of female wearing apparel, all have potential erotic values in the form of fetishes.

A woman's incidental side glance can be an intense stimulant, and is often so intended. Some men, on the other hand, may be attracted by malformations or perversions. The famous French philosopher, René Descartes, was powerfully attracted by crossed-eyed women.

See *VISUAL APHRODISIAC.*

Vocabula Amatoria

A French-English glossary of amatory terms occurring in Rabelais, Molière, Voltaire, and other French writers. The volume was published in London, in 1896.

Volatile Incense

In the Middle Ages perfumes and incense were used, in vaporous form, as atmospheric stimulants and adjuncts to sexual exercises.

Voluptuousness

To the Greeks, voluptuousness was a rule of life. A pupil of the philosopher Plato, a certain Heracleides Ponticus, author of a treatise *On Pleasure,* declared that voluptuousness in the conduct of life is a privilege of the ruling classes, labor being the fate of slaves.

The Greek poet Simonides wrote,

Would the life of mortals be delightful without sensual happiness?

Everything, therefore, that was conducive to the attainment of such an end was prized and lustily pursued.

Another Greek, the historian Megacleides, singles out Heracles as the supreme voluptuary.

Voyeurism

A sexually perverted condition that is believed to stimulate erotic desire.

The novels of the Marquis de Sade are full of descriptions of this perversion. In *Les 120 Journées de Sodome* a typical episode of this nature occurs. It is here reproduced in French,

Environ trois ans après que je fusse maîtresse de la Fournier, il vint un homme chez moi me faire une singulière proposition, il s'agissait de trouver des libertins qui s'amusassent avec sa femme et sa fille, aux seules conditions de le cacher dans un coin pour voir tout ce qu'on leur ferait.

See *MARQUIS DE SADE*.

Vulvae Steriles

The vulvae of the sow were popular as a gourmet's dish. Credited with erotic effects. Recommended by the poet Horace, Pliny the encyclopedist, and Apicius, author of a famous Roman cook book, *De Re Coquinaria*.

W

Waterfront Gaiety

According to the Greek historian and geographer Strabo, who belongs in the first century A.D., the city of Canopus, on the Nile Delta, was notorious for its festive indulgences. The traffic of ships on the canal between Canopus and Alexandria was incessant, day and night. There was male and female dancing on board the ships and in the nearby inns, to the accompaniment of wild sexual activities.

Water Lily

Monks, nuns, and clerics of all degrees used to drink daily, for twelve days on end, a concoction consisting of water lilies and syrup of poppies. This drink was believed to deprive the person who took it of any desire for sexual exercise. A similar anti-aphrodisiac, recommended by both Galen and Avicenna, was a hemlock poultice.

Water of Chastity

A seventeenth century recipe used in Germany as an anti-aphrodisiac. Among other ingredients, it contained absinthe, rue, camphor, coriander.

Wedding Dinner

On account of their popular repute as an aphrodisiac, mushrooms were served, together with pepper and pine-nuts, at wedding dinners.

Wedding Feast

A certain Macedonian, named Caranus, staged a lavish wedding feast at which female musicians imported from Rhodes appeared, so flimsily clad as to seem naked. Semi-nude girls, representing mythological characters, nymphs and

248

naiads, distributed silver candlesticks. The banquet, as usual, was a stimulating preliminary to more sexual entertainment.

Wells

In Biblical Shittim, immorality was rampant on account of the wells in the vicinity, called "wells of lewdness," because the waters contained aphrodisiac minerals. Numbers 25. 1-9.

White Wine

With juniper berries, Calisaia, which is a species of Peruvian bark, bitter quassia. The liquid is filtered and then mixed with bitter orange syrup. A glass, taken daily, acts in an amatory direction.

Whiting

Thought to contain aphrodisiac elements.
This is true of most species of fish.

Willow

The pounded leaves of the willow, drunk in a concoction, were formerly reputed to diminish amatory desires.

Wine

In Biblical literature, in the ancient classics, in the traditional mores of Europe and Asia, wine has uniformly been held in great esteem as a sexual provocation. From the most remote antiquity to contemporary times wine has been glorified in prose and verse. François Villon, that medieval Bohemian, favored hippocras as a drink conducive to laughter night and day, and sport and caresses and kisses.

A French song runs,
> Amis, pour bien chanter l'Amour
> Il faut boire,
> Il faut boire,
> Il faut boire,
> To hymn Love, my friends,
> You must drink, drink, drink.

Among the Romans, wine, taken in moderation, was considered an effective aphrodisiac. Petronius, in the *Satyricon*, writes,

I restricted myself to a moderate use of unguents. Then, adopting a more fortifying diet, that is to say onions and snails' heads without sauce, I also cut down my wine.

A common beverage credited with aphrodisiac virtue was old wine containing the pungent root of the plant pyrethrum or pellitory. So too with gentian wine, made from gentian root.

The Roman epigrammatist Martial emphasizes the need for moderation in wine drinking as a requisite for sexual indulgence,

You seldom drink a half measure of watered Falernian wine, Rufus. Did Naevia promise you a night of bliss and do you prefer the assured lubricities of fornication when you are sober?

Hindu rituals too condemn excessive wine drinking in amatory connotations. A drinking rule runs thus,

> So long as the steadfast look wavers not,
> So long as the mind's light flickers not,
> For so long drink! Shun the rest!
> Whoso drinks still more is a beast.
>
> Trans. by Mammatha Nath Dutt

In the eighteenth century the wines most in favor were, burgundy, port, and sherry.

The Marquis de Sade, in describing a meal whose primary function is voluptuous stimulation, lists, among the drinks, burgundy, claret, champagne, hermitage, tokay, madeira, Falernia. One of the guests, a duke, coolly drank three bottles in succession.

Wine and Love

Lucian, the Greek satirist of the second century A.D., in describing a festival in Asia, dedicated to Aphrodite, declares,

For more delightful is Aphrodite combined with Dionysus and both together dispense more delicious pleasure; but, separate, their enjoyment is less . . . Where the trees stood thicker and gave more abundant shade, welcome seats were placed, whereon people could take their meals; the towns-people, certainly, seldom made much use of them, but the great crowd (of visitors) enjoyed itself there and there rejoiced in all kinds of love-toying.

(Loeb Classical Library)

Winged Ant

During the Renaissance, the winged ant was used medicinally, it was sometimes also substituted for cantharides.

Witches' Techniques

The Middle Ages were permeated by the witch cult. Witches were consulted by love lorn maidens and swains, of all ranks and degrees. For their amatory ailments the witches provided strange pastes and potions and preparations that would, they promised, act as effective aphrodisiacs.

In some cases, witches were consulted to provide anti-aphrodisiacs to persons determined to oppose adulterous enemies or amorous opponents. Thus, in one of the major medieval expositions of witchcraft, the *Malleus Maleficarum*, The Witches' Hammer, by Heinrich Krammer and Jacob Sprenger, two Dominicans, there are discussions bearing on the power of the witch. The problem relevant to the issue under examination is whether, aided as she is by Satanic forces, the sorceress can bewitch the *membrum virile* and actually have the genitalia torn off by demoniac agency.

Witch-Hazel

Considered at one time as an effective erotic inducement.

Woodcock

The woodcock is not only a culinary delight but is reputed to increase seminal fluid.

Wormwood

In the Middle Ages, when sorcery and witchcraft were rampant, spells were frequently cast on a victim's potency. To counteract such a malefic condition, wormwood, a plant with a bitter taste, specially treated—in urina virginis sedecim annos mersa est—was used as a powerful antidote.

Worship of the Phallus

Among the Romans, Liber, *the God who Frees,* was a phallic deity. St. Augustine, who flourished in the fifth century A.D., describes, in his *De Civitate Dei,* the licentious nature of the cult. The genitalia were openly worshipped at the public crossroads. The phallus, displayed on carts, was borne through the countryside with clamor and excitement on the part of bystanders and worshippers.

In one town, Lanuvium, festivities lasted for an entire month. The rites involved sexual acts performed in public to propitiate the god, to the accompaniment of the most forthright and unbridled license of language.

Yet, for all their sexual and aphrodisiac features, the festivals were primarily directed apotropaically to avert sinister magic influences.

Y

Yarrow

This herb was much used by medieval witches.

For wedded couples, it was believed to ensure seven years' love.

Yeast

Used medicinally, also believed to possess amorous properties.

Yohimbine

This substance, derived from the bark of the yohimbe tree, is native to Central Africa. It is widely used by the Africans for its high sexual potency. It is also known as *quebrachine,* an alkaloid obtained from the bark of the *Quebracho.* The *Quebracho* is a large tree that grows in Chile, Bolivia, and the Argentine. Yohimbine is a yellowish powder. It has long been used as an aphrodisiac by the native tribes in South America and in West Africa. Its erotic potency produces its effect on the brain. It also stimulates the nerves of the spinal column which in turn stimulate the genitalia.

Z

Zola

Emile Zola, the nineteenth century French novelist, was remarkably sensitive to aromas of various kinds. His fiction is pervaded by this sensibility, particularly in regard to the *odor feminae*. In one instance he writes,

Everything exhaled an odor of woman.

One medical authority says, in reference to exhalations of various types,

Among animals, the connection between the olfactory and the genital organs is as incontestable as it is intimate.

SELECTIVE BIBLIOGRAPHY

Apuleius. *Metamorphoses.*

Bauer, B.A. *Women in Love.* Translated by E. and C. Paul 2 vols. New York, Liveright, 1943.

Bloch, Iwan. *The Sexual Life of Our Time.* Translated by M.E. Paul. London, Rebman, 1908.

Botkin, B.A. *A Treasury of Southern Folklore.* New York, Crown, 1944.

Brillat-Savarin. *Physiologie du Goût.* Paris, 1826.

Clauder, C. *De Philtris.* 1661.

Delrio, Martinus. *Disquisitionum Magicarum Libri Sex.*

Douglas, Norman. *Venus in the Kitchen.* London, Heinmann, 1952.

Egerton, C. Trans. *The Golden Lotus.* 4 vols. London, Routledge, 1939.

Ellis, Albert. *The Folklore of Sex.* New York, Boni, 1951.

Fassam, Thomas. *An herbarium for the Fair.* London, The Hand and Flower Press, 1949.

Finch, B. *Passport to Paradise?* New York, Philosophical Library, 1960.

Frazer, J.G. *Folk-lore in the Old Testament.* 3 vols. London, Macmillan, 1918.

Heartman, C.F. *Cuisine de l'Amour.* New Orleans, The Gourmets' Co., 1942.

Hirschfeld, M. *Sexual Customs in the Far East.* New York, Putnam, 1935.

Kiefer, Otto. *Sexual Life in ancient Rome.* London, Routledge, 1934.

Kruif, Paul de. *The Male Hormone.* New York, Harcourt Brace and Co., 1945.

Leyel, C.F. *Elixirs of Life*. London, Faber, 1948.

Licht, Hans. *Sexual Life in ancient Greece*. London, Routledge, 1932.

Martial. *Epigrammata*.

Meyer, J.J. *Sexual Life in ancient India*. 2 vols. Trans. by C. Egerton. London, Routledge, 1930.

Muller, Johannes. *De Febre Amatoria*. 1689.

Ovid. *Ars Amatoria*.

Remedia Amoris.

Petronius. *Satyricon*.

Pliny the Elder. *Historia Naturalis*.

Rompini, Omero. *La Cucina dell'Amore*. Catania, 1926. Somewhat in the manner of *Venus in the Kitchen* and *La Table et l'Amour*.

Sailland, M.E. *La Table et l'Amour*. Paris, Clé d'Or. 1950.

Schmidt, Peter. *The Conquest of Old Age*. London, Routledge, 1931.

Scott, G.R. *Encyclopedia of Sex*. London, T. Werner Laurie, 1939.

Scott, G.R. and Garland, P. *Sex and its Mysteries*. Westport, Conn., Associated Booksellers, 1955.

Scott, G.R. *Curious Customs of Sex and Marriage*. London, Torchstream Books, 1953.

Sinibaldus. *Geneanthropoeia*. 1642.

Stekel, Wilhelm. *Impotence in the Male*. 2 vols. New York, Boni and Liveright, 1927.

Thompson, C.J.S. *The Mystic Mandrake*. London, Rider and Co., 1934.

Van de Velde, Th. *Ideal Marriage*. London, Heinemann, 1928. Has been translated into many European and Oriental languages.

Venette, Nicholas. *Tableau de l'Amour Conjugal*. Spanish translation, Paris, 1826.

Walton, A. H. *Love Recipes Old and New*. London, Torchstream Books, 1956.